Sustainable Value

About the author

Chris Laszlo is the author of *The Sustainable Company: How to Create Lasting Value through Social and Environmental Performance* published by Island Press in October 2003 (paperback July 2005). A co-founder and partner of Sustainable Value Partners, he has trained thousands of *Fortune* 500 executives in "sustainability for business advantage" inside companies and at leading business schools around the world. He is a partner of Blu Skye Sustainability, the leading strategy consulting firm.

For nearly ten years, he was an executive at Lafarge SA, a world leader in materials, holding positions as head of strategy, general manager of a manufacturing subsidiary, and vice president of business development. Prior to Lafarge, he spent five years with Deloitte Touche consulting. Educated at Swarthmore College, Columbia University, and the University of Paris, Chris earned his PhD in Economics and Management Science.

He is currently Visiting Professor at the Case Weatherhead School of Management in Cleveland, Ohio, where he is also Associate Director for Corporate Strategy and Design at the Center for Business as an Agent of World Benefit. Since 2002, he has lectured at CEDEP, the executive education program in Fontainebleau, France, where he is a Visiting Scholar at INSEAD's Center for Social Innovation.

He is married and lives with his wife and two daughters in Great Falls, Virginia.

www.SustainableValuePartners.com

Early praise for *Sustainable Value*

"At a time when more and more business people are waking up to their contribution to environmental degradation and talking about the importance of moving toward sustainability, there is precious little in the business literature about *how* to do sustainability. Chris Laszlo has written a valuable guide that begins to fill the gap between talk and action. Read **Sustainable Value**, dispel the myth that environmental responsibility is expensive, and form a new vision of industry as part of the solution rather than a part of the problem; and more profitable at that, not less."

Ray Anderson, Founder and Chairman, Interface, Inc.

"Integrating sustainability into business activities is increasingly driving innovation and entrepreneurship. Global industry leaders are leapfrogging traditional EH&S and CSR approaches in favor of new business models that create value for shareholders *and* for society. **Sustainable Value** is a bold and inspiring read for managers who want the 'story' of sustainability as well as compelling case studies accompanied by a structured guide to managing in the new business context."

Luk Van Wassenhove, The Henry Ford Chaired Professor of Manufacturing, INSEAD

"Chris Laszlo's **Sustainable Value** is not only a great read but also a comprehensive and practical way for current and future leaders to learn to, as the book says, 'think differently' about the whole issue of ecological sustainability and corporate responsibility in practice. The work is engaging and the details provide a coherent and comprehensive picture of what it means to operate a profitable and highly successful business based on nature's principles with the future held clearly in mind."

Sandra Waddock, Professor, Boston College Carroll School of Management and Visiting Scholar, Harvard University

"In the swelling sea of sustainability literature, Chris Laszlo's **Sustainable Value** offers an island of clarity and focus. By combining compelling storytelling with actual cases and tools, he shows how mainstream companies can build competitively superior strategies by solving the world's social and environmental problems. Prepare to cast the 'trade-off myth' adrift once and for all."

Stuart Hart, S.C. Johnson Chair in Sustainable Global Enterprise, Cornell University and author of *Capitalism at the Crossroads*

"Chris Laszlo's message is huge and simple: we are on the eve of one of the greatest revolutions in management industry, an era of deep-seated transformation, where 'sustainable value creation' is emerging as the most powerful unifying thread for propelling industry-leading innovation in complete and simultaneous convergence with solutions to the call of our times. In *Sustainable Value*, Laszlo makes the vital point not with abstractions but with the real thing—for example, inside stories from the largest corporation in the world, and with frameworks, tools, and methods that take sustainable value creation out of the theoretical to the concrete."

Professor David Cooperrider, Fairmount Mineral Professor of Social Entrepreneurship, Weatherhead School of Management, Case Western Reserve University

"Chris Laszlo has done it again! He is challenging business and society to understand the ways in which businesses can use their core business strategies to act as agents of world benefit. The outcome? The economy thrives, businesses thrive, and society thrives. None of us knows enough about how business leaders could be contributing simultaneously to their own bottom line and to the common good. Using some of the very best case examples, *Sustainable Value* goes a long way in educating us to succeed in the 21st century."

Nancy J. Adler, Professor of International Management, McGill University

"Chris Laszlo recites numerous environmental and social challenges facing business, including those stemming from toxic chemicals in products. As a shareholder activist, I have witnessed many companies reaping benefits from stakeholder knowledge of such problems. But I've also seen companies ignoring stakeholder suggestions that could build enterprise value. My own involvement with the sustainable value network process outlined in *Sustainable Value*—which has led to Wal-Mart's adoption of a precautionary safer chemicals policy—convinces me that any business with a sizeable social and environmental footprint will need to apply Laszlo's tools if it wishes to provide sustainable value for shareholders and stakeholders alike in the years ahead."

Richard A. Liroff, PhD, Executive Director, Investor Environmental Health Network

"An accessible fable of a hard-nosed executive's awakening to the power of sustainability strategies to enable business success. The story, case studies, and toolkit convincingly reinforce each other to make the point that sustainability and business goals are a 'both–and' proposition not an 'either–or' trade-off. Chris Laszlo's first book, *The Sustainable Company*, should be a mandatory text in MBA schools. It now has a companion—*Sustainable Value* makes the theory come alive. I can't wait for the movie version, as a compelling response to the 'now what?!' question implied by *The Corporation*."

Bob Willard, author of *The Next Sustainability Wave* and *The Sustainability Advantage*

"Laszlo's latest book shows that the pursuit of shareholder value, corporate social responsibility, and sustainability are compatible and indeed complementary goals that make sense for the business mainstream. He includes valuable lessons for American business from the European experience, especially France, where CSR and sustainability are fully ingrained in the business culture. In a globalized world, American business must be ready to benefit from the lessons of others, or be doomed to incur the costs and repeat the mistakes of others by inventing its own solutions. *Sustainable Value* is squarely aimed at corporate America's bottom line and, in doing so, it offers business everywhere a roadmap to a better future."

Nicholas W.F.-R. Dungan, President, French-American Foundation

"Reinventing the role of business in society is the challenge addressed in this book. Companies now face a developing world with new stakeholders, organized without any real geographical boundaries and with added legal complexity due to new legislation. Companies can no longer afford to have a defensive and reactive role in which the pursuit of shareholder profit neglects the costs and injuries that business inflicts upon society. Society's trends generate new constraints but equally immense opportunities. In this context, business will need to collaborate with governments and civil societies in order to co-innovate and to answer the pressing, growing demands of a global world."

Claude Michaud, Emeritus Professor of Economics, INSEAD; Director General, CEDEP

"No less than the late and prolific management guru Peter Drucker has opined that all of our world's greatest challenges are business opportunities. Now comes *Sustainable Value* by Chris Laszlo, signaling a welcome shift from debate about Drucker's assertion to a grounded study of *how* managers and leaders can enable their businesses to flourish economically and become agents of world benefit. While this may appear a lofty and audacious aspiration, Laszlo's new work convincingly demonstrates the *knowledge and competencies* one needs to achieve it."

Ronald Fry, PhD, Chairman, Department of Organizational Behavior, and Editor, *World Inquiry on Business as Agent of World Benefit*, Case Western Reserve University

"Time and again innovative managers have shown that sustainable business practices are not only compatible with, but supportive of, strategic competitive advantage, and in ways that fit very different kinds of business strategies. While we know there is social *and* economic value in strategy that takes sustainability seriously, it isn't always easy to find. In *Sustainable Value*, Chris Laszlo shows us how, and in an eminently readable and compelling way."

Jonathan Johnson, Executive Director, Applied Sustainability Center, Sam M. Walton College of Business, University of Arkansas

Sustainable Value

How the World's
Leading Companies Are
Doing Well by Doing Good

Chris Laszlo

with a Foreword by Patrick J. Cescau, Group Chief Executive Officer, Unilever

Stanford Business Books
An imprint of Stanford University Press

Stanford University Press
Stanford, California

2 0 0 8

To my wife Lakshmi

Published in the USA by
Stanford University Press
Stanford, California

ISBN 978-0-8047-5963-2 (cloth)

CIP data for this book is available at Library of Congress

Published simultaneously in the UK by
Greenleaf Publishing Limited
Aizlewood's Mill
Nursery Street
Sheffield S3 8GG
UK
www.greenleaf-publishing.com

British Library Cataloguing in Publication Data:
    A catalogue record for this book is available from the British Library.

    ISBN 978-1-906093-06-8

Printed in the UK on environmentally friendly, acid-free paper from managed forests by Biddles Ltd, King's Lynn, Norfolk
Cover by LaliAbril.com

Contents

Business as an Agent of World Benefit: How the Holy Grail of business—
innovation—can be magnified through the power of sustainable value creation
Professor David Cooperrider, Founder and Chairman, Center of Business as an
Agent of World Benefit, with Ante Glavas, Executive Director, and Nadya
Zhexembayeva, Associate Director

Foreword

Patrick J. Cescau,
Group Chief Executive Officer, Unilever

There can be few people in business today who could doubt that social and environmental sustainability will be the defining business drivers for multinational corporations in the first part of the 21st century. This book serves as a timely reminder of the challenges and analysis of the opportunities this agenda presents to business, as well as a well-argued exposition of the need for companies to embed these issues into their business and turn them to their competitive advantage.

At Unilever we are fortunate in having a portfolio of brands that are intrinsically beneficial. Our foods brands provide basic levels of daily nutrition, while our home and personal care products not only help people clean themselves and their homes, they also play a vital role in delivering hygiene, sustaining good health and fending off disease.

We also benefit from being a company with a long history of social responsibility, so doing well by doing good, the subtitle of this book, has always been one of our guiding principles. Our 19th-century founders were socially minded business entrepreneurs who realized that margarine and soap, our first brands, had enormous potential to do good in terms of improving nutrition and raising levels of hygiene beyond the products' basic functional benefits. That potential is reflected in our culture and in our business mission today, which is to add vitality to life by helping people to feel good, look good, and get more out of life.

In the past it was sufficient for our managers around the world to use their individual judgment to decide on which societal and sustainability issues to tackle, based on local needs and, to a large extent, personal choice. In recent years, though, the globalization of our business, the massive changes the world is undergoing, the escalation of consumer concern about these issues, and the changing regulatory and political environment, have all prompted us to introduce a more formal process to integrate these issues into our business.

We have learned a number of things from this journey. Firstly, this agenda is not just about doing well by doing good. It is about doing better by doing good. It is no longer just about doing business responsibly; it is about seeing social and sustainability challenges as opportunities for innovation and business development. Rosabeth Moss Kantor, Professor of Business Administration at Harvard Business School, put it well when she said: "Companies that are breaking the mold are moving beyond corporate social responsibility to . . . social innovation. They view community needs as opportunities to develop ideas and demonstrate technologies, to find and serve new markets, and to solve long-standing business problems."

In other words, this is not only about product innovation or clever marketing. Sustainability enables you to think creatively and differently about every aspect of your business from raw materials to waste disposal. Take sales and distribution, for example. In 2002 we were confronted with the challenge of how to sell our products to the millions of people who live in small villages in rural India without any existing sales and distribution network. The solution our Indian business came up with was to create our own home-to-home retail operation from scratch by tapping into an existing social network of women's self-help groups and training women to become business entrepreneurs.

Today our rural operation in India is a multi-million-dollar business; it has created skills, incomes, and livelihoods for 36,000 women who were previously unemployed and living below the poverty line; it has brought products with nutrition and hygiene benefits within the reach of over three million households in 100,000 villages, many of them first-time consumers; and it has given us a market advantage our competitors will find hard to replicate. That is what I call social innovation.

The good news is that, as the breadth of case studies in Part II of this book highlights, the opportunity to turn societal and environmental challenges into opportunities for innovation and development applies to every business, be it a construction materials firm, the world's largest retailer, a chemicals corporation, or a packaging company.

A second important consideration has been the insights we have gained by looking at our business through external eyes. As a consumer goods company, it is our brands that drive our growth, so the process we introduced to integrate social, economic, and environmental considerations into our business is brand-led. As with the Sustainable Value Toolkit described in Part III of this book, our process spends as much time looking at our brands from the outside in as it spends considering inside-out factors. It is crucial, in our experience, to consider all the external influences on a brand, from what issues consumers are concerned about, to the forces shaping this agenda from a regulatory, competitive, and trade perspective, to the views of external stakeholders. As this book recommends, it is particularly valuable to listen to the opinions of a broader set of stakeholders, be they celebrities, journalists, academics, or NGOs, because what they say, write, lecture, or campaign about today tends to be what consumers will be concerned about tomorrow.

Thirdly, this agenda allows no short cuts or half measures. As sustainability moves center-stage and the "conscience consumerism" movement gathers momentum, it can be tempting for companies and brands that have not got to grips with this agenda to go for a quick-fix solution or an advertising-led approach. They are then surprised to find that they are roundly attacked for "greenwashing" or for trying to obtain a disproportionate amount of kudos for their efforts than the benefits of their actions actually warrant.

That approach no longer works, if it ever did. Today, companies and brands can succeed only if they are *genuinely* values-led and take a holistic rather than silo approach to social, economic, and environmental issues. That is why, even if you don't communicate everything you do, you have to have a sustainability point of view on every aspect of your value chain and every step in your business life-cycle.

Fourthly, working with others achieves better results. Businesses can often be extremely well placed to tackle social challenges, as Chris Laszlo rightly argues, but business cannot and should not attempt to take them on alone. In many parts of the world, for example, we fortify foods with micronutrients to help tackle iodine, iron, and vitamin deficiencies, a major cause of ill-health and arrested development. This has a significant impact on public health, but we cannot take on the wider health and social implications on our own, which is why we work with Unicef and local health services on the ground to achieve long-term sustainable progress.

Similarly, our Lifebuoy soap brand is working with others in India and Bangladesh to reduce death and disease caused by diarrheal infection by teaching families about the existence of germs and the importance of washing hands with soap at critical times of the day. Over three million people a year die from diarrheal disease, mostly children, and research shows that handwashing with soap can cut that number by half. But, however successful we are with Lifebuoy's hygiene education program, which aims to reach 200 million people over five years, we cannot tackle this huge social challenge without the involvement of local government, NGOs, and international health and welfare agencies.

Fifthly, companies need to move quickly to gain competitive advantage. Unlike some aspects of product development, this is not an area that can be easily copied or fast-tracked, so the sooner companies apply the principles set out in this book the better placed they will be. Many of the business costs that are currently outside the immediate control or scope of a business, such as raw material and waste disposal costs, are likely to become much bigger factors than in the past as global shortages take hold and "polluter pays" legislation is introduced. Companies need to plan now to mitigate the effects of a future where resources are under threat and externalities have to be paid for.

So the message is clear. Companies that successfully embrace this agenda and integrate it into their businesses and brands will thrive. Those that fail to do so, or react too late to the dramatic social, economic, and environmental changes that are taking place in the world, risk becoming corporate casualties.

Finally, for most of us in business, sustainable development resonates with our personal values. A business that puts this agenda at the heart of its business mission and culture will recruit and retain people with the right mind-set to tackle these issues because, at the end of the day, we all want our lives to have a higher purpose and we all want to see a better world. Or, as John F. Kennedy once said, "In the final analysis, our most basic common link is we all inhabit this small planet, we all breathe the same air, we all cherish our children's future and we are all mortal."

Foreword

Tyler J. Elm, Senior Director,
Corporate Strategy & Finance, Wal-Mart Stores, Inc.

As you read this book, you will discover that many global businesses are on a journey towards business sustainability, not as an environmental initiative, but as a business strategy that derives economic value from the pursuit and achievement of enhanced social and environmental outcomes. Chris Laszlo illustrates how the competitive strategies of some of the world's largest mainstream businesses are changing as their leaders begin to take on a number of the world's most important social, environmental, and economic issues such as climate change and ecosystem health. In doing so, he asks us to consider the drivers of corporate and competitive strategy as well as what has changed to account for this broader scope for business in civil society. But when did this change happen, and why?

Each of us is likely to have different answers to these questions based on our own personal experience and journey. I recall a colleague presenting me with the following statistic a few years ago: "Of the world's 100 largest economies, 42 are now corporations, not countries." This statistic made us stop and think, and helped create the context for our journey towards business sustainability. For Wal-Mart Stores, ranked first on the *Fortune* 500 and approaching $350 billion in annual sales by 2007, it contributed to the framing of the opportunity represented by sustainability and, for me, it served as a personal mile marker on that journey.

We incorporated the statistic into presentations on sustainability to peers, senior executives, and the Board. For comparative purposes, we included our estimated rank at the time—20th—coming in just after

Sweden's gross domestic product. Collectively, the organization began to ask itself two important questions:

- What will be the role of business in society during the 21st century?

- What will it take for our company, in every country where we are present, to continue growing at current rates for the next 20 years?

And then, Hurricane Katrina made landfall in the United States. My wife and I had just moved from the Florida coast—four days before Hurricane Rita, and after Hurricanes Frances and Jean. I remember being glued to the television, watching the aftermath unfold in Florida and across the Gulf as this latest storm passed. We watched in disbelief as traditional public institutions failed to meet the needs of their citizens while individuals, non-governmental organizations, foundations, and big business responded in their stead to provide food, water, and shelter. Wal-Mart was one of the many that responded to fill the void, and I was proud of "my" new company and colleagues.

After Katrina, those two questions came up again and again at our company, in meeting after meeting, in presentation after presentation, shaping our sustainability strategy. And our CEO, Lee Scott, presented us with another: "What if the very things that many people criticize us for—our size and reach—became a trusted friend and ally to all, just as it did in Katrina?" Soon after, on 24 October of that year, Lee took the company's business sustainability strategy public with his unprecedented speech: *21st Century Leadership*.

However, what was happening at Wal-Mart Stores was not unique. Indeed, we were "Johnny-come-lately" to sustainability and so we sought the insight and experience of others—thought leaders from academia, governmental and non-governmental organizations, think-tanks, suppliers, and our suppliers' suppliers.

Indeed, many large mainstream companies were already acting on the business opportunities created by a knowledge-based economy in which civil society plays a more active role with correspondingly higher socioeconomic expectations and an unprecedented ability to organize enabled by the World Wide Web. In the wake of weak public institutions, these businesses were responding to emerging market mechanisms and legislation designed to target the growing divide among socioeconomic expectations and their (non-)fulfillment. However, what was different than even a few years previous was that some of these companies were connecting sustainability to their core business activities. Their managers were starting to incorporate sustainability into key decisions on which businesses to enter and how to compete.

These managers are now beginning to play a leading role in solving some of the world's toughest problems because they can do so while earning a fair profit. In the process, they are developing new relationships, knowledge, and competencies as they respond to value propositions defined by a broader set of stakeholders with pressing social, economic, and environmental needs. And many are finding that they can better serve their economic *and* societal stakeholders by re-examining the very business activities that define their organizations today. These business leaders are learning their way into a new mode of operation, tapping new sources of value, and, through the journey of business sustainability, developing new sources of inimitable competitive advantage.

In my case, I had not detected this change as a competitive force outside of the natural resource industries and industrial products companies until 2003. By 2004, it was an emerging strategy among a few mainstream consumer businesses. By 2005, I found myself in the middle of an effort with the world's largest company as it applied the principles of sustainability to its core business in its quest to become an even better company. But what was driving this change in competitive strategy? Was there more to it than risk management and process efficiency?

Less than two years after first coming across the statistic that would serve as a personal mile marker and while killing time by reading as I waited for a plane that should have come and gone three hours earlier, I again came across that statistic, only it had changed: "Of the world's 100 largest economies, 51 are now corporations, not countries." It was the last weekend in March 2007 and, as before, the statistic was already outdated. I remember thinking "business has reached the tipping point" as I considered the happenstance of having embarked on our sustainability strategy at that time—as the wealth of nations and the political economy that was birthed during the industrial revolution pivoted on a fulcrum. Would it redefine itself in the process? How soon after the tip would momentum follow? How will business redefine itself in the global socioeconomic network that is today's global economy?

While we may not be able to provide definitive answers to these questions, I challenge you with the following question: Do you really think the role, or even the expectations, of business in society will be the same in the next 25 years as in the last?

If you answer "no," then I urge you to consider the corporate culture within which you work and how it might best adapt to significant change in the social expectations and economic opportunities that affect the very decisions of what businesses to enter and how to compete. Do you, or your organization, have the competencies, skill-sets, and networks that will enable you to take advantage of such change? At Wal-Mart Stores in early 2005, the answer was "no." However, our sustainability strategy provides us with a gateway to becoming an even better company because it enables Wal-Mart to develop the managerial competencies, skill-sets and organizational networks that we will need to take advantage of the increasingly networked, global political economy.

In short, my learning was this: in addition to the economic value derived from the outcomes themselves, the process of "learning-by-doing" through collaborating with multiple and diverse stakeholders changes the way we work. The experiential learning that comes from examining value chains and developing strategy within a collaborative network of external thought leaders generates value for the business by further developing personal and organizational perspective, systems thinking, and an enhanced awareness and understanding of the external business environment. In doing so, managers and their organizations develop the means to incorporate this enhanced world-view into decision-making and business activities. Similarly, non-governmental stakeholders are better able to address the systemic challenges of society, and to replicate and scale desired outcomes. In the process, they often end up taking approaches and organizational models more typical of social entrepreneurs.

While we are still picking low-hanging fruit, if the early results of Wal-Mart's business sustainability strategy are any indication, these organizational capabilities and processes—and the managerial and leadership skills—will prove to be a phenomenal source of inimitable competitive advantage. The value of sustainability as a business strategy is not what is written on a whiteboard or the scribbling on the back of a napkin. It is the value of developing prepared minds, and the ability of an organization to incorporate innovation into the corporate culture. Ideas are inert; people make the difference, and culture eats strategy for breakfast every day.

In summary, we are witnessing a metamorphosis in the role of business in society, with for-profit companies targeting many of the emerging social issues once reserved for the non-profit sector. Friedman's edict (that the business of business is business, and the creation of shareholder profit its fundamental mandate) is just as true now as it ever was. Yet what *has* changed is the context within which business operates, and thus how one applies this edict. The sources of value available to business and the competitive forces acting upon it continue to change; they are different today compared with 1982, and they will be different yet again in 2032. And so we should not be surprised by shifts in the sources of business value, or by changes in the business activities required to deliver a winning value proposition.

Perhaps it is merely the cumulative inertia of our institutions and the busy work of "heads-down" execution? Perhaps it is the discontinuity of such change with our own personal understanding of business models and our individual experience of what has worked in the past? Regardless, the notion of a static socioeconomic and environmental context for business—with unchanging sources of value and stagnant preconceptions of the very role of business in society—is absurd when viewed in the abstract and even more so when viewed in retrospect.

Peter Drucker may have said it best: "Every single pressing social and global issue of our time is a business opportunity."

Introduction

Sustainable Value is divided into three parts. Part I is a management fable about Deena, a young CEO, and the challenges she faces to profitably address her company's impacts on society and the environment. Her story is one of personal empowerment, of finding balance and connection to what is important in life. It's also a tale of corporate profit and growth.

What makes Deena's story unique is that her eventual success—personal, financial, and corporate—is the result of "doing good." She is a talented but ordinary human being who demonstrates leadership in a time of heightened global problems ranging from poverty to the energy crisis and climate change.

In telling her story, I've drawn a composite picture based on business leaders I've been fortunate to know and work with over the past 25 years. These corporate chieftains face many challenges in their personal and business lives related to a world deeply in crisis. A small but influential group, they are now reinventing the role of business in society. They are shifting the focus away from minimizing negative impacts (such as brutally downsizing employees or unintentionally contaminating soil and water) to offering new solutions to global problems that the public sector has been unable to tackle alone.

Part II outlines the new competitive environment in which societal challenges are becoming huge business opportunities. It showcases mainstream global industry leaders who are successfully integrating sustainability into their core activities, not only from a sense of moral correctness, but because it makes good business sense. In the new competitive environment, stakeholder value—based on the economic, ecological, and social impacts a company has on its diverse constituents—is becoming a way to achieve competitive advantage. Issues such as climate change and global poverty are introducing greater levels of complexity into strategic decision-making and often have far-reaching implications for companies in today's competitive environment.

The real-life sustainability stories of DuPont, Wal-Mart, Lafarge, and Cargill's NatureWorks are guided by top management with profit and loss responsibility. Unlike smaller niche players in the 20th century, they do not rely solely on a visionary founder—nor do they depend on the director of sustainability—to "green" the company or to adopt greater social responsibility.

As industry leaders with tens of thousands of employees and businesses that span diverse supply chains across the world, these companies seem incapable of being paragons of virtue. Their blemishes and occasionally deliberate mis-steps, such as Toyota's push into large gas-guzzling SUVs[1] in the same time-frame as their roll-out of the hybrid drivetrain, are part of their quest for competitive advantage in markets that still reward short-term shareholder value even if it incurs a substantial cost to society. But, warts and all, these behemoths promise a renewed relevance for business in society: they represent the most powerful institution on Earth shaping a better future for everyone, everywhere.

Part III offers a toolkit and process for mainstream business managers who want to know how they can take advantage of the new competitive environment. It provides a guide to creating shareholder *and* stakeholder value in a broad range of sectors. Taking advantage of sustainability as a new source of competitive advantage requires a change in the mind-set of leadership and a disciplined approach to integrating stakeholder value throughout the business. This section of the book introduces "sustainable value" as a distinct approach to managing value creation. It provides a step-by-step approach—based on delivering consulting engagements and hundreds of executive working sessions in *Fortune* 1000 companies—to building sustainable value inside large complex organizations. It is designed to help managers identify how and where they can do well by doing good—providing the practitioner with the means to compete effectively in the 21st century.

Who should read this book and why

There are two target audiences for *Sustainable Value*. The first is young people everywhere who, in contemplating a career in business, want to succeed professionally while feeling that they can make a difference. *Sustain-*

able Value provides them with a positive image of the future in which business success and contributing to a better world can go hand in hand. It shows them how corporations can be an agent of world benefit. The second audience is mainstream business managers who may not know what environmental and social sustainability has to do with job performance, and are looking for a credible and realistic introduction to the topic.

There are a growing number of well-written books on sustainability in business. They include those on its theory and practice filled with insightful analysis supported by detailed case studies:

- *Walking the Talk: The Business Case for Sustainable Development* by Chad Holliday, Stephan Schmidheiny, and Philip Watts[2]
- *Capitalism at the Crossroads* by Stuart Hart[3]
- *The Next Sustainability Wave* by Bob Willard[4]

Many are scholarly, such as:

- *Green to Gold* by Daniel Esty and Andrew Wilson[5]
- *Competitive Environmental Strategy* by Andrew Hoffman[6]
- *Down to Earth* by Forest Reinhardt[7]

Others are practical field guides, such as:

- *The Sustainability Handbook* by William Blackburn[8]
- *Leading Change toward Sustainability* by Bob Doppelt[9]

In contrast to this book, all are academic works geared to readers who, at some level, already buy in to the concept of sustainability. None is accessible to an intelligent and skeptical general public, or to a busy line manager who knows little about sustainability and wants a quick yet incisive introduction without the MBA textbook experience. This book was conceived to be accessible to the general public, while being credible and compelling to the hard-nosed business executive.

Acknowledgments

I'd like to begin by thanking those who helped bring to light my previous book, *The Sustainable Company: How to Create Lasting Advantage through Environmental and Social Advantage* published originally by Island Press in 2003 with a paperback edition in 2005. All of them contributed in some way or another to this work. Background material for *Sustainable Value* was researched in collaboration with current and former executives at Toyota, Lafarge, Wal-Mart, DuPont, Orange (France Telecom Group), Interface, NatureWorks, Aviva, Unilever, Patagonia, Green Mountain Coffee Roasters, Intel, Saint-Gobain, Renault, Verizon, Fairmount Minerals, Celanese, Weather-chem, First Energy Corp, and many other companies—some of which are true sustainability leaders and others who are struggling simply to find a way forward. I owe a special debt of thanks to my colleagues Dave Sherman and John Whalen, who co-founded with me Sustainable Value Partners, Inc. They and colleagues Jib Ellison, John Buffington, and Marc Major all played key roles in Wal-Mart's leadership on environmental sustainability between 2004 and 2007. Their insights and experience have been invaluable. Any mistakes and inaccuracies in telling the veiled Wal-Mart and Interface stories that appear in Part I of this book are mine alone.

A special word of thanks goes to Jean-François Laugel, former partner at Corporate Value Associates and current founder of A & F Conseil, as well as to Alban Aucoin, Federico Balzola, Laurent Guy, and Michael Heurtevant. They are close colleagues and friends for over two decades who have helped to shape my vision of business and society.

Bertrand Collomb, the chairman and former CEO of Lafarge SA, the world's largest cement and construction materials company, modeled sustainability leadership throughout his extraordinary career, which included chairing the World Business Council for Sustainable Development. He continually inspired me during the nearly 20 years I've had the privilege to know him.

Professor Stuart Hart, currently the S.C. Johnson Chair of Sustainable Global Enterprise and Professor of Management at Cornell University's Johnson School of Management, provided unparalleled thought leadership on business sustainability long before it became fashionable. He is a true pioneer of sustainability strategies for the mainstream business community. His 1997 *Harvard Business Review* article, "Beyond Greening: Strategies for a Sustainable World," winner of the McKinsey Award for best article, helped me make the decision to abandon my more traditional business career in favor of research, consulting, and teaching in this field. His spring 2007 invitation to me to teach a class in his sustainability course at Cornell was a pleasure and indeed honor for someone who has followed in his footsteps.

In a similar vein, Ray Anderson, the founder and chairman of Interface Inc., helped lead the early way, with a system-wide transformation of a billion-dollar industrial company into a model of sustainable enterprise, and with an impassioned plea for business leadership in service of "tomorrow's child." His readings of the early drafts of the manuscript, and his generous and thoughtful feedback, were invaluable to the book's final form.

CEOs and senior corporate leaders Patrick Cescau, Lee Scott, Jeffrey Immelt, Dennis McGrew, Bob Stiller, Didier Lombard, Matthew Kiernan, Hewson Baltzell, Nicole Notat, Chuck Fowler, Jennifer Deckard, Andy Ruben, Tyler Elm, Paul Tebo, Dawn Rittenhouse, and Olivier Luneau all contributed immensely to my thinking and, in many cases, directly to the ideas and content in the chapters ahead. In addition to generously writing a Foreword to this book, Tyler Elm is a principal contributor to the Wal-Mart chapter.

Academic leaders and senior professors David Cooperrider, Ron Fry, Mohan Reddy, Nancy Adler, Luk Van Wassenhove, Sandra Waddock, and Rosina Bierbaum have provided exemplary thought leadership on sustainability as a management topic. David Cooperrider and Ron Fry's seminal contributions to Appreciative Inquiry (a whole-system strength-based approach to change) has deeply influenced the way business leaders approach stakeholder engagement on complex sustainability issues.

For inspiring conversations over the years and help in generating visionary ideas, I would also like to thank Mark Milstein, Ante Glavas, Nadezhda Zhexembayeva, Loïc Sadoulet, George Eapen, Jens Meyer, Joseph Rinkevich, Daryl Banks, Bob Faron, Herbert Fockler, Nicholas Dungan, Mike Bertolucci, Bob Willard, Rick Fedrizzi, Hunter Lovins, Santiago Gowland, Emma Stewart, Rick Ramirez, Susan Anderson, Susan Svoboda, Eileen Claussen, Rob Lebow, Todd Baldwin, Art Kleiner, Ira Feldman, Lavinia Weissman, Dan Sayre, Allen Hammond, Monica Tousenard, Meredith Myers, Dennis Church, Leslie Pascaud, Al Segars, Katie Kross, Jean-Yves Larrouturou, Gentiane Weil, Joel Luboff, Tidiane M'Baye, Alessane Dienne, Carina Van Vliet, Adrian Payne, James Blakelock, Maggie Parker, Jia Feng, Jon Johnson, Tom Davis, and Chuck Bennett. My family is populated with its own thought leaders on sustainability—many thanks go to Lakshmi, Jenna, Ishana, Alexander, Kathia, Sastry, Kalpakam, Carita, and Ervin.

Special thanks goes to John Stuart, managing director at Greenleaf Publishing, and to Dean Bargh, its editorial director, and Bill Gladstone, my agent, head of Waterside Productions, Inc. They provided wise counsel and valuable editorial guidance in crafting early versions of the manuscript.

A key challenge is how to communicate the concept of sustainability. People everywhere find it difficult to imagine that they have abundant opportunities to make the world more sustainable without having to sacrifice professional success or personal fulfillment. Teaching the topic to executives—particularly senior executives and line managers who are inclined to be highly skeptical about any silver linings in intractable problems—has been a fruitful way to trial the messaging of this book to its target audience. I would like to thank INSEAD Professor Claude Michaud, Dean of the CEDEP Executive Education program, for giving me the opportunity to teach a course on "Sustainability for Business Advantage" several times a year since 2002. In the US, Professors David Cooperrider, Ron Fry, and Betty Vandenbosch at the Case Weatherhead School of Management gave me an opportunity to begin teaching the material in their executive education program. Professors Stuart L. Hart and Al Segars at Cornell and UNC Chapel Hill, respectively, gave me similar opportunities in their MBA programs.

Chris Laszlo
Great Falls, Virginia
November 2007

Part I
Deena's story

If people do not revere the Law of Nature,
It will inexorably and adversely affect them.

If they accept it with knowledge and reverence,
It will accommodate them with balance and harmony.

Lao Tsu, Tao Teh Ching

1

Life at the top

Deena Marstreng's phone rang. It was the Governor of Illinois, whom she had met at a recent museum fund-raiser. "Deena, I'd like to invite you and your husband to a private dinner at my home. The Vice Premier of China is visiting next month and I'd like you to be part of our informal welcoming committee." Deena smiled. She would offer to give the Chinese leader a personal tour of downtown Chicago in her new black and silver Hummer.

The meeting that morning with the analysts had gone as expected and the financial markets were once again bullish on her company—a chemicals and materials giant—mostly on the strength of her business unit's performance. Sales and growth had exceeded expectations. Deena knew that the distribution costs of the Midwest region could be lowered still further—a move she hadn't yet shared with her boss or with the analysts. She relished being a star performer, loved being able to exceed expectations, and drove herself and her team hard to do so quarter after quarter.

Five years earlier, at the age of 27, Deena had been appointed general manager of the business unit inside the corporation. No one in the 100-year-history of this blue-chip company had risen so fast at such a young age. Inside the giant multinational, Deena was the chief executive of a business with thousands of employees and factories on three continents. Arriving at seven o'clock each morning, Deena oversaw every aspect of the unit's expanding global operations, often finishing late at night so that she could speak to her plant manager in Nanjing before the Chinese day began.

Now, taking in the view of Michigan Avenue and the vast lake from her corner office, Deena felt a deep sense of satisfaction. She was one of the most highly paid executives in her company, with a stellar executive assistant who helped her life run like clockwork. Facing her desk and across from the private conference table with seating for 12 people, visitors could settle into one of four butter-soft leather Milanese armchairs around the Noguchi coffee table. Outside work, she made up half—or by some accounts a bit more than half—of Chicago's pre-eminent young power couple, with a social entourage of statesmen, politicians, and executives of leading corporations.

Her business unit was a highly profitable producer of lightweight plastics, manufactured composites, and industrial non-woven fabrics. The transportation sector—mostly cars and trucks—represented nearly a third of annual sales. Deena hired talented people and then helped them reach their full potential, setting clear goals, and working hard to make sure everyone could reach them. Her team of senior executives included Janice in Sales & Marketing, Prakash in R&D, Maxine in Human Resources, Josh in Legal, Roberto in Operations, and Andy, her Chief Financial Officer (CFO). The culture of the business unit was no-nonsense but friendly. Everyone knew they could make it if they worked hard and delivered bottom-line results.

From day one, Deena had methodically built up a high-performance organization. She had a compelling strategic vision for the business and set extraordinarily high profit targets for the years ahead. Her ability to execute on the vision was equally impressive. It soon became apparent that financial results for the business unit were firmly on track relative to the targets. She had the full confidence of her boss, Scott Giffen, the company's CEO. Word around the water-cooler was that she was being groomed to replace him when he retired.

Blindsided

Three years after her appointment as general manager and despite her team's slick new corporate social responsibility (CSR) report, the company was ranked 23rd out of 25 peer firms on a list of "Best Environmental and Social Companies in the Specialty Materials Sector." The ratings were compiled by an investment agency that specialized in evaluating blue-chip companies on their environmental and social performance. The evaluations were then sold to fund managers to help them manage their investment portfolios.

In the ratings commentary, Deena saw that her business unit was being singled out for its industry-high levels of greenhouse gas emissions, the health risks arising from toxic chemicals in its products, supply chain issues related to human rights abuses in Asia, and the low wages paid to its hourly staff.

In reality, few mainstream investors paid attention to this kind of information and the news wouldn't have been half as bad if it hadn't appeared in a USA Today sidebar titled "Corporate Citizens—Worst Offenders," prominently mentioning her company by name. Among the unpleasant fallout of the negative publicity was the growth in proxy statements filed at the Annual Shareholders' Meeting in which activists demanded that management commit to reduced greenhouse gas emissions and use of toxics, and to greater transparency on employee compensation and human rights issues.

In another surprising development, Deena learned that her business unit was being targeted by two international non-governmental organizations (NGOs)—ProtectEarth and Human Rights Assurance International (HRAI). Both groups were publishing inflammatory pieces that reappeared regularly on a growing number of activist Internet blogs. One article in particular caught her attention. It urged investors with a social conscience to avoid holding her company's stock. Then someone sent her anonymously a YouTube video that parodied the company's leadership to the tune of Gloria Gaynor's "I Will Survive" with a polluted and over-crowded Earth crashing down on her avatar.

The final straw was a call from Maxine to say that they had lost a key candidate for the new senior marketing position, a very highly qualified graduate of Deena's Alma Mater, the Stanford School of Business. The reason the candidate gave for rejecting the job was the unit's poor corporate citizenship. He had a choice of employers and didn't want to work for an organization with such a negative image.

Deena decided it was time to act on these simmering issues. She called Michael Reinford, head of Human Rights Assurance International and a vocal critic of her company.

"Michael, this is Deena. You came to my office a year ago to talk about a supplier called Venkata Ltd. You were concerned that our purchases of semi-finished goods from them appeared to condone their human rights abuses. I'd like to get your assessment of the progress we've made since then, not only on human rights but on all the social and environmental issues we face. I'm looking for an off-the-record exchange of ideas to help me understand our situation better from your perspective."

There was a long pause on the other end. Though Michael sensed the sincerity in her voice, it was highly unusual for a chief executive to call him for any reason other than to give him a verbal thrashing.

Deena pressed ahead: "Would next Wednesday around one in the afternoon work? I'll come to your New York head office."

The following Wednesday, Deena was ushered into well-appointed offices at a prestigious address on Manhattan's upper west side. Wood paneling and floor-to-ceiling windows might have led the casual observer to mistake the offices of Human Rights Assurance International for those of a thriving law firm. Deena waited in a large conference room as a ceiling-mounted video projector covered one wall with images of women and children working in obviously abusive conditions in Afghanistan, Brazil, sub-Saharan Africa, China, and—to her surprise—Germany and the United States.

"These activists try to make business responsible for everything that's wrong with the world," she thought as the disturbing images flashed by. "But they've never run a business. They have no idea what it takes to run a company. Why can't they see the good we're doing? Social problems are for governments, not corporations, to solve."

A dialog begins

Michael Reinford walked briskly into the conference room and, after a few pleasantries, got straight to the point. "Today, your company has a very poor image with socially conscious investors and with activists like us. It's an image that's rapidly moving into the public eye thanks to media pieces like the one in USA Today. Your business unit is considered one of the worst offenders. It's highly energy-intensive and fossil-fuel-dependent. You release nearly a ton of greenhouse gas for every three tons of products you produce. Your manufacturing uses chromium and antimony oxides, lead chromate, mercury, and other highly toxic chemicals like benzene. Forty per cent of your employees are hourly and paid the minimum wage. Two of your plants are in parts of the country where the cost of living is too high to raise a family on the minimum wage, which means that you fail to pay these workers a living wage."

Deena was disturbed, but also secretly impressed by his knowledge of the facts.

He continued: "In the molding process used by your industrial clients to manufacture car parts, your products off-gas several dangerous chemicals including known carcinogens. You have hundreds of raw materials and equipment suppliers, most located in developing countries. Many of these suppliers are known violators of human rights, yet you have no system in place to ensure that violations don't occur. In spite of your own rise to the top—which we applaud—fewer than 15% of your employees are women, less than 7% of your corporate staff are minorities, and you make no provision for handicapped employees at three of your primary facilities."

Deena carefully worded her response to avoid conceding anything. "I understand that environmentalists and social activists have a problem with how we do business—in fact, they seem to have a problem with business in general. What I don't understand is why the blame is being put at our doorstep. Everything we do is within the law. We comply with all existing standards for environmental and social performance, and we apply American standards overseas even when we aren't required to do so. For example, the product off-gassing you mentioned occurs under carefully controlled conditions and is well under legal limits. This happens at our client facilities, so we aren't required to know this, but because we care, we do. And we know, as you are also undoubtedly aware, that there is no medically proven health risk at current levels of off-gassing."

"The issue isn't about legal compliance," said Michael. "Doing just what the law requires is no longer good enough," he added flatly.

She tried another tack. "I think the main problem may be that we've communicated too little too late about the good things we do. As you've seen, this year marks the beginning of our environmental and social reporting. Our CSR report describes where we are making progress. For example, it showcases the solar energy installation at three of our facilities. One of our plastic compounds is now used in the casings for wind turbines. We are adopting a new environmental management system at every manufacturing site. Also, we've published a code of ethics that we require our suppliers to adopt if they want to do business with us. We're very surprised at the low rating we received this year and plan to be more active in promoting our efforts in the future."

Feeling that she had defended her point, Deena stood to fill her glass of water. She was all the more surprised by what she heard next.

"Don't think I'm unsympathetic, but I must tell you that communicating isolated instances of corporate responsibility is unlikely to make a difference. What you are doing is what many people would call *greenwashing*. The cases in your CSR report are either superficial or they are exceptions to the norm. They mask the real damage being done by your core business.

"Your internal reporting structure sends the same message—it reflects how little strategic importance your business unit attaches to corporate social responsibility. Instead of reporting directly to you, your CSR manager reports to Human Resources. And the CSR report itself is heavily a product of the CSR manager's collaboration with outside consultants rather than with internal business teams. The report is supposed to be a thoughtful self-assessment and plan for improvement. But how important can this process really be to your business when your regular employees are barely involved? How much impact can it possibly have when consultants drop off their recommendations at the door of the CSR manager and say: 'Here you go . . . See you next year for more of the same?' "

Deena paused to reflect on this. Then she remembered she had sought out this critic in the hope of learning something. So, rather than defend herself further, she decided to ask for Michael's advice. "If you were in my shoes, what would you do? What actions would you take to convince an organization like yours that we are sincerely committed to running our business without these growing legal and public relations hassles?"

Michael looked up at her and sighed. "Given how you are thinking about the problem, I can't think of any actions you or your managers could take that would make a real difference. You would first need a different set of values and principles by which to act. You would need to see the world differently."

"What on earth is he talking about?" thought Deena. "He sounds like some New Age guru. '*See the world differently*.' What does that mean?"

She tried one last question. "Just what values and principles are you referring to? My job—and my team's job—is to earn a profit for our shareholders. When we do this successfully and within the limits of the law, we create jobs, we contribute to economic growth, and we give the buying public what they want. What better values are you proposing?"

"I'm sorry but I can't give you the answer you're looking for," said Michael. "That will take a journey of discovery on your part. I can tell you that it won't be an easy journey or a quick one either."

Deena stared at him. "Well, how does it begin?"

"The road is different for everyone. If you're committed to making a difference, you'll find the right place to start."

Growing more frustrated, Deena tried once more. "Well, how would I know if I were on the right path?"

After brief reflection, Michael told her simply, "Be authentic and look for integrity and coherence in yourself and in the world around you."

None of this was making any sense and Deena suddenly felt precious worktime slipping away from her. Her East Coast plant managers meeting on labor productivity was scheduled to start in an hour in neighboring Murray Hill, New Jersey. She thanked Michael graciously, promised she would ponder what he said, and left.

Deena fights back

At the next Executive Team meeting, Deena took an aggressive stance on the recent environmental and social challenges they were facing. "We can't afford any more negative publicity. It's alienating our clients, demoralizing our staff, creating a confrontational atmosphere at our general assembly with shareholders, and it's already tripled our legal expenses. Soon I'll be spending a quarter of my time on lawsuits. It's a waste of scarce resources! We have to fight our critics and the media on their grounds. We'll prove that what we are doing is scientifically safe from a health and environmental perspective. We will sue anyone who asserts fault on our part without legally valid proof."

There were mumblings of agreement from around the table.

"All of you need to help make the case for corporate responsibility, but don't give away the store," she added somewhat cryptically.

Privately, Janice asked Deena if a deeper problem didn't exist. "Our newly hired CSR manager, Art, isn't changing a thing around here," said Janice. "None of our business managers pay any attention to him. What if we need to rethink some of our processes or product designs from an environmental or social perspective? One of our big clients in Sweden told me last week that our competitor there has started reformulating its compounds and coatings to include an environmental dimension at every step of the way—from the choice of raw materials to production processes and product disposal."

Deena stared out the window. "Janice, our operations and products are never going to satisfy the tree huggers of this world. Most of our critics don't understand business and they want us to do things that would lead to financial losses. Now that would really be socially irresponsible! If we lose money, it'll destroy jobs and eventually take a valuable set of products off the market, or leave someone else to supply them and that someone would probably incur a heavier environmental and social cost than we do."

Looking glum, Janice said nothing. Her passion for the environment was something she had learned to keep to herself. A little-known fact about her was that she had a PhD in paleoclimatology. She also served as a volunteer in her spare time on a national science committee on climate change—something she didn't dare mention to her boss. At times like these, it was an impossible challenge to separate her private passion for the environment from her professional obligations as head of Sales & Marketing.

The next morning, Deena called Maxine, Art, and her legal head Josh, into her office. "I've allocated half a million dollars in next year's budget to lobbying government to slow the growth in environmental regulations. I've also hired a public relations firm to work with you, Art, on local community relations at all our plants and to strategize with Maxine on improving our labor relations."

At the next meeting with financial analysts from Wall Street, Deena made special mention of her business unit's sharp focus on cash flow.

"We can't afford to be distracted in today's highly competitive markets," she told the analysts. "We face criticism by environmentalists and social activists, but we don't expect to lose any significant business on their account. The worst thing we could do is to compromise our product excellence by adding costs to satisfy a few extremists. We are one of the world's leading plastics and coatings companies, and we intend to continue that leadership within the framework of the law." She received a standing ovation and the following morning her company's stock was up a hundred basis points.

But non-governmental organizations continued to attack. The occasional defamatory article in the press was either retracted or met with positive coverage under the watchful eye of her lobbyists and legal team. By December, her company's stock was selected along with the worst environmental performers in the oil & gas and chemical sectors for inclusion in the Vice Fund—founded on the idea that "sin" stocks such as tobacco, armaments, and adult entertainment were highly profitable activities that yield above-market financial returns to investors.

Some considered the Vice Fund selection a dubious honor. Deena didn't care one way or another as long as profits continued to rise. Janice, on the other hand, submitted her resignation shortly before Christmas.

Earnings continue to grow

That fiscal year proved to be a banner one for Deena's business unit. By year end, the category "lightweight plastics, composites, and industrial non-woven fabrics" was the biggest financial earner for the company. The successful acquisition of a low-cost Chinese competitor had expanded their client–service capabilities and, along with the sinking of a mid-size competitor in central Europe, made the company the world's second largest player in its sector. The restructuring of her East Asian operations added another ten million dollars to the bottom line. And, perhaps most significant for Deena personally, a major new product design on which she had gambled heavily generated a 20% jump in profits.

All this lent an air of inevitability to Deena's promotion to executive vice president (EVP) of the company. Becoming EVP entitled her to stock options that made her a multi-millionaire on paper, as well as a seven-figure cash bonus which she used to open a trust fund for her twin boys. This would eventually guarantee them financial freedom for life. It also led Stanford to invite her as commencement speaker for that year's graduating MBA class.

While she knew she should have been thrilled by her rapid, inexorable rise, it all left her feeling vaguely uneasy. A walk down the eighth-floor corridor—the "hall of power" in her company—now earned her a wide berth from most of her colleagues, who either feared her or showed excessive deference. The quarterly dance with financial analysts was becoming a tired one. The need to make every year a landmark year, to deliver blockbuster products in stagnant markets, to continually lower costs and outcompete rivals, no longer thrilled her as it once did.

For reasons she couldn't quite understand, her organization had lost some of its zest. People worked hard and knew that delivering good results meant good pay and career opportunities. She was proud of the culture of excellence—researchers, salespeople, accountants, plant managers, foremen, order clerks, and legal staff who did extraordinary work in service of the company. But she sensed that their motivation extended to little beyond stock options and an annual bonus. There was no passion, no pride, and none of the ownership culture and drive to create a promising future that permeated the division when she first started. Watercooler conversation seemed increasingly focused on what was wrong with the company rather than what was right.

Her family life also suffered. She could count in minutes, not hours, the time she spent with her husband during the week. Her once vibrant social life and her time with the twins were relegated to a few weekend hours a month.

All this, she calculated, was the price of making it to the top. It was a price she thought she could live with.

Settling in at mid-career

Over the next few years, much of her business unit's day-to-day operation was turned over to Andy, her able chief financial officer. She knew Andy hoped one day to succeed her at the helm. Her numerous duties as group executive vice president included heading the Growth Excellence Committee and the Compensation Committee, and traveling to meet line managers around the world, sharing her vision of the company's future and inspiring the troops. She often represented the company or accompanied CEO Scott Giffen in meetings with financial analysts or in large-client negotiations, even when these involved other business units within the company.

She was also occasionally subpoenaed in court to defend the company against allegations of misconduct ranging from the forced displacement of a Hmong village in Thailand during the construction of a new ethylene plant to a groundwater contamination accident that poisoned parts of an ethnic-minority neighborhood near Houston, Texas.

Hitting rock bottom

Deena, now in her mid-thirties, was already an old hand at the corporate game when the first major economic downturn struck. A recession in the auto markets combined with a sharp rise in key raw material and energy costs—much of it oil-related—squeezed profit margins. Ironically, the company was now so well-managed that further cost reductions or efficiency gains were difficult to come by, leaving little room to maneuver. Sales continued to fall, month after troubling month.

In strategy sessions across the company, senior managers tried to figure out the extent of the damage. They hired management consultants to conduct market and competitive analyses. Prakash reported on new product development in R&D. The new head of Sales & Marketing forecast aggressive sales projections for the next three years.

When all the reports were compiled, Deena was asked to assemble the data and recommendations into a briefing for Scott Giffen to present to the Board. Her prognosis for the company was not good. All major financial indicators were low and falling. Only two significant product innovations were expected in the near term. The company was losing market share to Chinese competitors with lower overhead and pension costs. Indonesian and Brazilian companies were entering the market with radically lower-priced products and, when they eventually solved their quality problems, they would begin to nibble away market share. In short, Deena concluded in her briefing, the good times were over.

Shortly afterwards a dramatic memo began to circulate: hiring and salaries would be frozen until further notice. Whispers in the hallways suggested that bonuses were being eliminated and layoffs could soon follow.

Deena drove herself hard. A working week of 60 hours became 80 hours as she toiled to squeeze costs, accelerate innovations, and extract maximum value from every company asset, including its people. Members of her team who didn't measure up to the new expectations were quickly let go. For the first time in her career, she felt overwhelmed, unable to get the results she wanted. Deena resolved to do something about it. Soon.

2
Turning point

The flight back from the Frankfurt analysts' meeting was scheduled to leave shortly. Scott Giffen was not in a good mood and Deena wasn't looking forward to spending eight hours with him in the cabin of the company's private Gulfstream IV-SP jet. International operations had missed their financial targets for the third consecutive quarter. With sales down and financial liabilities growing in all areas of the business, the meeting with the Deutsche Börse analysts had been particularly brutal. This time, Scott was likely to face growing Board pressures to turn things around or leave. As they settled into the aircraft's plush leather seats, Scott ordered a double whiskey. Deena looked away as he gulped down half of it, his eyes glazing as he stared out of his oversized panoramic window.

"We'll just have to tough it out," he said. "Oil prices can't stay this high forever. They're bound to come down soon. Car sales in China are going to continue growing in the double digits. We'll see an up-tick in our sales before long."

Deena wanted to agree with him, but the economic news seemed to be getting only worse. They were no longer competing on a level playing field. As a *Fortune* 500 company based in the United States, they had huge costs related to labor and increasingly to waste management, pollution control, and product toxicity. They spent a small fortune each year documenting their operations and products to show that they complied with a rising number of environmental laws and regulations, including the new and onerous EU chemicals legislation REACH. She knew their competitors in China and other emerging markets had far fewer costs in these areas. It was beginning to seriously hurt the bottom line.

The flight would normally have been a great opportunity to bring up the subject of her vacation. Deena hadn't taken off more than a week in the last two years. Still, she hesitated to mention time off. Everyone in the Executive Group was putting in extra hours and, for the time being, vacation time was not exactly a hot topic. Finally she said, "Scott, I'm going to take two weeks off in August. It's on the calendar and Andy is fully up to speed on what needs to be done in my absence."

Scott didn't say anything for what seemed like a very long time. "Where are you planning to go?" "Yellowstone Park," she replied immediately. "The boys have been researching it for a school project."

The opportunity to leave the downtown traffic, the airports, the office buildings, and the crowded city streets for the wide open spaces of Wyoming sounded like just what the doctor ordered. She would begin planning the journey that same night and would ask her secretary to book the flights in the morning.

The trip west

A month later, the flight from Chicago through Minneapolis touched down in beautiful Jackson Hole, Wyoming, a frontier town at the foot of the Tetons and the Gros Ventres mountains. Her husband Matt and the kids grabbed homemade ice-cream at Moo's in the back of the Beaver Creek Hat and Leather store on the main square, while Deena studied the route north into Yellowstone. The August weather was cool and dry at 6,200 feet. Before long they were on their way in their rented Cadillac Escalade, heading up through the Park's southern entrance into bear and bison territory.

On their first day in the park, Deena was up well before dawn. She still had jet lag from her last trip to Europe. The time difference and the lingering stress from work left her wide awake at 3.30 in the morning. Matt and the kids would probably sleep until eight, so she left them a note and hopped in the Escalade. She decided to drive toward Ridley Lake where she had heard bears could often be seen in the early morning hours. Parking the car at the trail head, she decided to be adventurous and head out by foot toward the lake's edge, leaving as the first signs of morning lit the eastern horizon.

The near-dark 20-minute walk to the lake was an astonishing experience. The first thing she noticed was the complete absence of the sounds she had lived with every minute of her life—the cars, trucks, planes, trains, and other clatter of civilization. Next she felt the moist earth beneath her feet, saw the huge domed sky with the morning's last bright stars, brushed against the wild trees and leafy shrubs, and stared in amazement at winding river valleys exactly as they must have looked 5,000 years ago.

Looking back on the last few years, Deena felt a tug of sorrow. How rarely had she been able to experience such a deep connection to nature and to the world around her! Here she was, alone, slightly scared, wondering if a bear would surprise her around the next bend. Yet she felt also strangely exhilarated. It was as if her animal mind could savor a prehistoric connection to the earth, a bond that her ancestors had known every day but that her own life had denied her.

A chance meeting

When she reached the water's edge, she discovered she was not alone. Seated on a fallen tree trunk was a man, perhaps in his early thirties, wearing a legionnaire's hat with a small backpack by his side. Squinting into binoculars, he seemed completely absorbed by what he was seeing. She started to say something, but stopped when he gestured for her to remain still. "Shhhh," he whispered. "Don't make any noise."

She held her breath and tried to see what he was looking at in the early morning haze. Then she saw it—a pack of grey wolves, with a leader more massive than any German Shepherd dog she had ever seen.

"Here, have a look," he said as he passed her the binoculars. "Over there, on the far side of the lake."

Deena took the binoculars and saw that a herd of elk had come to drink. The bull had a 12-point set of antlers. The rest seemed to be cows and calves. She swiveled back to look at the wolves. While the elk hadn't seemed to notice the wolves yet, the wolves had taken a predator's laser-like interest in the herd.

Awed to have stumbled on this scene on her first morning out, Deena wondered out loud, "Are the wolves going to catch the herd?"

"Maybe, maybe not," said the man. "That's what I love about this place. There's such a finely tuned balance to it. Every morning a wolf wakes up in this park knowing it will have to outrun an elk in order to eat. And every morning each elk knows it will have to outrun a wolf to survive. Neither can win all the time. If the wolves always won, there would be no elk. And if the elk always won, they'd overrun the place. It's part of nature's subtle dance."

Uh-oh, thought Deena. This guy sounds like a real tree hugger—probably another Michael Reinford, working to save the world from the ills of civilization. She shifted the conversation to more familiar ground.

"It's quite a change for me to be here. I'm usually stuck in the office or at the airport." She added almost apologetically, "I work for a big multinational."

"Me too," he said to her surprise. "My name is Doug, by the way. From Arkansas. I'm here with my wife and daughter." He held out his hand.

"Deena. Pleased to meet you. My family and I are staying at Grant Village. What do you do when you're not on vacation?" she said with a laugh as she realized she was starting to enjoy the conversation.

"I'm president of the apparel division of a global retailer," he said.

Deena nearly fell back in surprise. Her expression must have given her away.

"I bet you thought I was an environmentalist," he added with a smile. "Actually I run a billion-dollar business. The decisions my company makes influence a whole range of industries that supply to us from across the world including China."

"My company is a global leader too," said Deena thinking how funny it was to have a China connection out here in the middle of Wyoming. "But recently it seems that we've become stuck in a rut. We've had losses for six straight quarters in a row. Speaking of environmentalists, we're getting slammed on all fronts. It's starting to really burden us. I'm spending a lot of time and money defending the company against lawsuits and negative media coverage."

Doug gave a small but kind smile. There was a short lull in the conversation as a young Sandhill crane made its languid way across the lake.

"Let me tell you the story of how my company is handling environmental and social challenges," he said with a glint in his eyes. "You can believe me when I say we've had lots of experience in this area!"

Something told Deena the next few hours would be out of the ordinary. She sat on another log a few feet away and listened as Doug began.

The retailer's tale

"Several years ago, we were getting hammered by social activists. There were lots of reasons, some real and others imagined—exploiting immigrant workers, low wages, union busting, sexual discrimination, unpaid overtime, driving out small businesses, destroying the fabric of local communities, outsourcing jobs, and human rights abuses. You name it, we were being blamed for it. The worst part is that many of the accusations were right on target. But our management was hunkered down in totally defensive mode, just trying to weather the criticism and keep on generating the profits we were accustomed to. It wasn't that our management was badly intentioned. It's just that we had a different logic for the social good we were doing, like putting money back into the pockets of rural American middle-class families.

Diving off the Cocos Islands

"Then a fortuitous event took place involving our largest individual shareholder—he's a member of the family that founded the company—and a leading environmentalist. The two of them were on a trekking expedition to biodiversity hotspots like Madagascar and islands off the coast of Costa Rica. It provided just the right backdrop for conversations about how industry often unintentionally destroys delicate habitats—from the stunningly colored coral reefs they saw while diving to the rainforests of Scarlet macaws and Mollucan cockatoos.

  "Somewhere along the way, our shareholder realized that his company was in a position to make a huge difference because of its global reach. He saw that it could be a driver of change to protect and even restore the dwindling natural environment. But he had no idea if it could work as a way to run a business. Plus, he wasn't part of the executive team, so all he could really do was make the right introductions between his environmentalist friend and our current CEO.

Getting a head start

"The timing was good. Our CEO, Rick, was dealing with new lawsuits every day, with negative media pieces that were really starting to hurt our public image. Many of our employees were feeling unsure about working for us. They felt that they were being treated like pariahs in their local community. Some of our customers—while they were always happy with our low prices—were beginning to have a problem with the 'bad guy' image. We were starting to worry about consumer boycotts."

Doug explained that, as a huge multinational company, they were bound to be targeted sooner or later by anti-business activists.

"Rick understood that most of the lawsuits and pressure groups were focused on our social problems. Environmental problems hadn't really started in the retail sector. When he finally met with the environmentalist leader, Rick thought, why not get a head start? Why wait to get attacked on environmental issues? Instead he decided the company needed to figure out what exposure it had *before* environmental issues became a business problem.

"We quickly realized that we knew very little about our environmental impacts. We wanted to start with a risk assessment. We wanted to know how much downside our company really faced on the environmental front. Then Rick met an outside consultant, not the usual run-of-the-mill kind who either focused exclusively on financial performance or on advocacy for the environment. He understood the relationship between business and the environment. I remember the consultant kept telling us the same thing at the beginning: *'Environmental sustainability is your ultimate form of competitive advantage.'* "

"We couldn't really understand what he meant by this. He kept saying that environmental strategies were the biggest business opportunity of the 21st century. He seemed a bit over-zealous, but he seemed also to understand our business and could relate well to Rick and the senior exec group. So we decided to take a chance on working with the guy.

Sizing the company's footprint

"The consultant and his team started us off with an assessment of our existing environmental impacts—our environmental 'footprint.' Like footprints in sand, the things our company does and the products that we sell each day have an impact on the environment. The footprint we leave behind includes the waste we throw out, the water we use, our energy consumption and CO_2 emissions, and the health impacts of our products. He convinced us that we didn't need to do a detailed footprint analysis, only enough of one to get a general sense of our exposure.

"In retrospect, when we started to look at our environmental impacts, we didn't believe they were that significant. It turns out that our company's footprint is actually quite large when you compare it even to national environmental footprints. Most of our environmental impact is in the products we buy and sell, not in our own store or fleet operations. It's in our supply chains."

Figuring out what it means

Deena found this fascinating, but difficult to put into perspective. How big a problem were all these environmental impacts?

She asked him, "You talk about environmental impacts. But how do these things affect people's health and the reliability of your product supply? Aren't those the real business issues? Otherwise environmental arguments end up sounding simply like they are against progress in general. They might even sound like they are against jobs and the welfare of the poor people that environmentalists claim to be so worried about."

"That's true," said Doug. "And we've reached the point where most of these environmental impacts *are* leading to big health problems. They *do* affect the reliability of supply of many of our products. For example, water scarcity is a huge and growing problem where people don't have access to safe drinking water. Water contamination contributes to more than half of all infant deaths in countries where we're increasingly doing business. Many of these same water sources are used to grow crops that we sell as foods or the fibers that are used in our clothing products. As a global industry leader, we can't hide behind our suppliers when they have negative health impacts in the process of growing and manufacturing our products."

A morning breeze turned the lake's surface alive with ripples where it had been smooth as a mirror moments before. Deena skipped a few stones along the shoreline, thinking about her own company's relationship with suppliers such as Venkata Ltd.

"Toxins in foods and common household products are leading to cancers, neurological damage, enzyme disorders, and other illnesses," Doug continued. "The loss of topsoil from over-farming means it is increasingly difficult to feed the world's growing population. The loss of rain forests and falling biodiversity means fewer new medicines. Local air pollution contributes to asthma and respiratory diseases."

He paused. "I could go on but I think you get the picture." Deena nodded, keenly aware of nature's untouched beauty all around her. The sun's early morning rays had just begun to appear over the treetops. "Everything you say may be true," she said as she skipped a stone that left a perfect trail of ever smaller splashes on the lake's surface. "But look at all the positive contributions a company like yours makes."

He smiled at the turn in the conversation. She continued, "By making merchandise widely available at low cost, you're helping to reduce poverty. You're making it possible for the average person to live a better life. In fact, companies like yours contribute to higher life expectancy and better health for people everywhere."

"Yes," he said. "You're right about that."

"As for the environmental and health problems you described," she added, "won't business find solutions for most of them? Human ingenuity always finds a way. Just look at the new technologies we're developing, from nanotechnology and genomics to biotechnology."

This time he took a moment longer to respond. "Business can be part of the solution to the world's growing environmental and social problems. But technology alone won't be enough. Business—especially global industry leaders—needs to see the world differently."

Deena had a sudden flashback to her conversation with Michael Reinford. *See the world differently*. Here was that phrase again. She was feeling caught once again in the debate between business and environmentalists. "Can we walk along the lakeshore?" she asked. Doug readily agreed as they began to walk side by side along the wide path of sand and beaten earth.

The visionary's vision

"So how did you and your CEO defend your company against social and environmental attacks?" she asked.

"We didn't," replied Doug. "A lot of people thought our critics just wanted to shut us down, but eventually we realized a lot of those criticizing us were not entirely unreasonable. They never see all the good we do, it's true, but they generally don't just invent things out of thin air. Many of them were customers we were slowly alienating, and we didn't recognize this until it was nearly too late."

"Eventually, we learned the hard way that when a lot of different people see the same problem, they may have a point. So, after a lot of pounding in the press and from Wall Street, we started listening more. And we stopped trying to minimize environmental and social problems."

"Most of all, we realized we could never win if all we played was defense. So we shifted our focus away from CSR and public relations, and decided to make our business managers directly accountable for environmental performance as a driver of business performance. Our strategy now is to work with our customers, suppliers, NGOs, and many others to *profitably* meet our environmental and social challenges. The results of our efforts are reported in our main annual report, not in a separate CSR report that no one reads."

With sudden misgivings, Deena thought about her decision to hire Art, a former ad man, and to put him in a public relations role centered on CSR reporting.

Doug continued, "Early on, Rick made the unusual move of holding an off-site meeting with 25 of his key line managers to learn about the environmental issues of the 21st century, how these might affect our company, and how our company might affect them. Based on the environmental footprint analysis, his executive team began to see that topics such as water supply, soil, fisheries, and energy were not just environmental issues but key business issues that threatened our ability to serve customers in the future. In that meeting his team decided that, despite everything else on their platter, environmental sustainability was something that warranted our further attention."

Asking the right questions

"The next step was to reach out to environmental activists—not militant ones that wanted to see us fail at any cost, but constructive ones who were interested in moving markets in a positive direction—plus government officials, academics, and others in order to expand our company's knowledge of specific environmental challenges. This outreach really helped to shape our new business strategies. Each of a dozen teams was asked to develop innovative leadership strategies in which our company would reinvent itself with environmental sustainability at the core of our new business model. The objective was to leverage our company's ingenuity, scale, and scope to create extraordinary value for the business and for the environment."

Doug could sense that Deena was getting a bit overwhelmed.

"Look, it was really pretty simple." He stopped to face her directly. "By asking questions such as 'How much of a building's energy actually delivers value?' 'Why can't our trucks get better mileage?' 'Why does organic cotton cost twice as much?' we were able to get breakthroughs that we hadn't gotten before in how we design our products and purchasing. We saw things that we hadn't been able to see before. We then got Board approval to move forward with business sustainability as a core thrust for the entire company. It became the next 'big idea'—a way for us to continue growing and to generate above-average profits."

"That really is impressive," said Deena. "But how did you get your team engaged in the first place? Weren't they overwhelmed with short-term objectives that prevented them from wanting to take on these additional environmental targets?"

She looked across the lake as she thought of her own overworked organization.

"Good question," replied Doug. "The success of our strategy was in no small way dependent on sustainability's galvanizing effect on our buyers and suppliers. Once engaged in the quest for a more sustainable product, these managers brought new levels of creativity—and passion—to their jobs. Performance became no longer just about profit, it became about creating financial *and* societal value. Believe me when I say that every one of our employees—no matter what their political, social, religious, and other views—wants to contribute to a better world if given half a chance."

"But how did you get people to buy in to sustainability in the first place?" persisted Deena, not satisfied with Doug's answer. "I mean, it's not just a logical issue, is it? Don't people have to get it at a gut level? Isn't the environment an emotional issue above all?"

"You're absolutely right," nodded Doug. "One of the most powerful ways to engage people was what we call 'eat what you cook' field trips. Let me tell you a little about these trips.

The cotton fields of San Joaquin

"We took our key managers—even our CEO—to see first-hand what impacts our business was having on nature and society. We visited land-fills on the East Coast, mountain tops in the Rockies, supplier factories in China, and, in the case of the cotton used in the manufacture of our clothing apparel, we went to the San Joaquin Valley, home to more than a million acres of cotton farms."

"You were betting that, for most people, seeing is believing," observed Deena.

Doug nodded. "Let me try to share with you what our trip to the cotton fields was like. It was two years ago in June. Getting out of our cars at one particular field, we got to see first-hand what looked like essentially a scorched earth. The farmer who arranged the tour, a member of the Organic Exchange, a non-profit that promotes organic cotton, explained to us that the soil on this conventionally farmed cotton field was chemically sterilized and served as little more than a structural support for holding the crop stems upright. Seeds are fumigated to prevent fungi. Herbicides eradicate the weeds and pesticides exterminate the insects.

Synthetic nutrients feed the plants. Other chemicals regulate plant growth and the speed of opening of the cotton bolls. Defoliants are used to kill the plants and get rid of the leaves at the time of harvesting.

"In fact, as our guide was explaining this to us, a small single-engine plane flew low over the field, spraying a soft cloud of chemicals that began a slow drift towards us. We were back inside our cars in a few seconds flat!

"Then, on our way back, we drove past a storage shed with dozens of barrels of chemicals—mostly empty—some laying on their sides, some split open. Just then two children riding bicycles were cutting across a nearby field. As we got out of our cars to look for someone responsible for the storage shed, I walked over to the path the kids had taken and leaned down to touch a bent wet stalk of corn. My fingers started to burn. It was unbelievable. That's when I really started asking myself what kind of world my company was a part of. Even if we weren't directly responsible for this mess I was horrified to think that in some way we were playing a role in it.

"We talked to farmer groups including some who had chosen to switch to organic methods. We met third-generation farming families who had a statistically very high count of cancers across the generations of men who worked the fields, and who switched because of that. We met community leaders who spoke about poisoned wells and accidental deaths from chemical exposure on the fields. And we heard from biologists who described the devastation to local ecosystems in the valley, and the disappearance of bird and small animal species."

"I had no idea that cotton had such problems," said Deena at she stared up at the sky, still dark blue and clearing in the early morning light.

"To get back to your question," Doug continued, "it's useful but it's not enough for people to 'get it' on an emotional level and to want to be environmentally responsible. Obviously, as I'm sure you realize, there has to be business logic.

Why it makes sense for business

"The business case for organic cotton was actually as persuasive for us as the environmental case." Doug began to enumerate the ways on his fingers. "Product differentiation with consumers is the most obvious: at the same color, style, quality and price, the organic cotton seal becomes a 'plus one,' particularly for higher-income shoppers who come into our stores just to buy this type of product. Secondly, we have reduced risks from tightening environmental regulations of toxic chemicals, reduced community and NGO opposition, and an enhanced image for us with employees and external stakeholders. Thirdly, we have the opportunity to change the business context of the entire apparel sector. By helping to make organic cotton competitive with conventional cotton, we are helping to revolutionize mainstream consumer expectations with a first-mover advantage based on establishing loyal relationships with farmers and other players who hold the key to organic cotton as a scarce resource.[1]

"We are now expanding our range of organic cotton clothing apparel: bedsheets, towels, ladies' wear, baby clothes—even teenage fashion. And, believe me, it's not just us. The whole market is growing fast. Retail sales of organic cotton have more than doubled in the last four years."

Further illumination

"How unique an example is the cotton story?" asked Deena. "I mean, it sounds really good. But you can't tell me that the majority of the products on your shelves have an environmental problem for which a solution exists that's good for the customer, good for profits, and good for the environment."

"Actually, you'd be surprised," replied Doug. "The cotton example is not at all an isolated example of a win–win for business and society. Many of the negative environmental and social impacts in our supply chains have technical solutions that are also economically attractive. In some cases, it requires a redesign not only of the product but of our entire value chain, so we have to take a whole-system approach. The real issue in most cases is not whether a solution exists or whether a business case can be made. It's about mind-set. It's about making people, including our customers, aware of what is possible.

"Think of the common household light bulb," he continued. "The kind with a thin filament that glows is incandescent. You could replace it with a compact fluorescent bulb (CFL) that costs ten times more but lasts ten times longer. So, in effect, the purchase price over the life of the bulb is the same. If you did replace the incandescent bulb with a CFL, you would end up also saving between $30 and $80 on electricity bills because a CFL uses 80% less electricity. It's an economic win for you, the consumer, and a win for the environment: one CFL swapped out for one incandescent bulb prevents 500 pounds of coal or one barrel of oil from being burned, and it keeps a ton of greenhouse gas out of the air. So why wouldn't you? It's a product that requires no sacrifice—you save money and you save the world."

"Sure," said Deena, trying not to smirk. "I remember one of those U-shaped bulbs in my father's basement. I hated it. It took ten seconds of flickering before it turned on, made a noise like a crazed insect, and had a cold white light."

It was Doug's turn to smile. "Yeah, I remember those." He paused thoughtfully. "But today's CFLs are a completely different thing. They're virtually indistinguishable from incandescent bulbs. They're bright, white, steady, and silent. You should try one when you get home.

"So the question is, why aren't we making the rational decision to go out and replace our old bulbs, when they burn out, with new CFLs?"

Deena's answers came in rapid fire: "Because we didn't know they existed in their improved version. We just never thought about it. We've always bought the same old thing. They're only available as a specialty item in the store that I go to. And anyway what difference does a light bulb make?"

At the last comment, Doug raised his hand to halt the discussion. "Now that's an interesting question: what difference does it really make? Can replacing one light bulb with another have any kind of real impact? Well, we asked ourselves that very same question. The answer astonished us. It turns out that if each of our customers changed just a single light bulb from incandescent to CFL, it would save over $3 billion on electricity bills over the life of the bulb. It's the equivalent of preventing 50 billion pounds of coal from being burned and that, in turn, is the equivalent of taking out two million cars' worth of greenhouse gases from our air for an entire year. And, because CFLs last on average for eight to ten years instead of less than a year, it would also keep one billion bulbs from being landfilled.

"By the way, there are lots of other products in exactly the same situation—sustainable fisheries that cost no more than the unsustainable ones that deplete our oceans, consumer goods packaging that decomposes in nine years instead of nine million years, trucks that get twice the fuel efficiency of standard fleets, stores and buildings that give back to nature while being lower-cost to operate than their traditional counterparts. The real question for business is not whether the technology exists or whether a business case can be made. It's whether the mind-set exists to even see these opportunities in the first place. You have to know how to look at your business with new eyes."

She looked at her watch and suddenly realized two hours had gone by. It was nearly 7.30 in the morning. With a few words of thanks for a truly extraordinary conversation, Deena began her jog to the car. She made it back to her family by eight, arriving at their cabin just minutes before they stirred.

The rest of her vacation was spent getting much-needed rest and going on meandering hikes with husband and boys in tow. She saw Doug one more time, waving to her from across the dining room at the main visitors' building.

"You see that man over there in the legionnaire's hat?" she said to Matt and her boys just as they were finishing their desserts. "His company wants to be recognized for helping the environment—not just for energy efficiency and things like that, but for improving our quality of life. Can you imagine a business model like that?" she added with a smile.

"You mean your company doesn't contribute to making the world a better place?" asked one of her twins. Out of the mouth of babes, thought Matt. He saw her wince before changing the subject.

On the flight home, Deena reflected that the conversation with Doug left her feeling uneasy but also hopeful that she might one day embark on a new path—one that would allow her to turn her company and her job into something that she could be proud of for herself and her children.

3

Rebirth of the sustainable company

On her first morning back in the office, Deena had to deal with all the usual fire-fighting that piles up after vacation. She was also determined to put into action what she had learned during her break. She was now convinced that there had to be a better way to run her business, if for no other reason than her company's continued mediocre earnings and the growing business risks related to its social and environmental problems. At 10 am, she reached for the phone and placed a carefully thought-out call to Janice asking her to come in to discuss a possible rehiring opportunity. Deena knew that without Janice's knowledge and vision it would be difficult to move her team forward on sustainability.

Now it was time for her impromptu staff meeting to begin exploring a new way forward with her team. After jotting down a few notes, she walked down to the main conference room to find Andy, Maxine, Prakash, Roberto, and Josh already seated.

Deena engages her team

Deena sat down and began with a factual review of the environmental and social issues the company was dealing with: high levels of greenhouse gas emissions and fossil fuel use; allegations of unfair labor conditions; human rights abuses by suppliers; toxic chemicals at manufacturing sites; and class-action lawsuits accusing the company of contributing to increased health problems near the sites. Using slides and financial tables, she put these issues in terms of business costs and lost opportunities. "We've lost at least 10% of our business from customers who are electing not to buy from us because of our reputation as a top polluter and socially irresponsible company," she commented.

Although the team had heard her speak before about environmental and social issues, they were surprised by the change in her tone. Gone was the defiance, the denial of responsibility, and the rejection of accusations by NGOs and the media as being unfounded. Even more surprising to them, Deena shared her experience of meeting Doug, whom she described as a divisional CEO of a global retailer that had addressed sustainability issues from a business perspective and made money doing it. While her intention was to simply relay the experience of another mainstream company, Deena's eyes watered momentarily as she made the plea for sustainability as "a smart business decision but also the right thing to do for future generations."

There was some banter back and forth, reflecting edginess as the team collectively pulled its thoughts together on an unfamiliar topic. It was not the usual focus on earnings targets, PR campaigns, or hiring and firing. Deena could sense the frustration and skepticism in the room, but also a faint inkling of motivation and the renewed energy to accomplish something really worthwhile. That inkling was enough for her. She knew then that the team would eventually find value in a continued exploration of sustainability as a business opportunity for the company.

Janice's return

The next day Janice came in for the meeting that Deena had requested. She was surprised and pleased to hear Deena say, "You were right about the environment being a strategic business issue for us." "You know I'm working for one of your competitors now," Janice replied. Deena assured her that she did and was interested in a conversation about "a leadership role that I think you'll find compelling."

It had been a while since Janice submitted her resignation. Deena began to fill her in on the downturn in the business, the missed quarterly earnings, and the falling stock price of the company. She shared her own disappointment and growing loss of excitement for her job over the last six months. It was altogether a gloomy picture. Janice wondered how this conversation could possibly lead to a career-enhancing opportunity. But it became quickly apparent to Janice that Deena's thinking about sustainability had gone from abstract enigma to something very different—guttural, urgent, and no longer possible for her to ignore.

"Janice, a growing number of mainstream companies are struggling with environmental and social pressures. What strikes me as fascinating about the best of them is not that they've taken a different or more aggressive approach to environmental and social issues. It's that they are using environmental and social issues to reinvent their businesses. They're playing offense."

Deena went on to share her growing epiphany that sustainability was an opportunity for the company, a way to become competitive that wasn't about fighting in the red ocean of today's mature markets but instead about competing in a blue ocean of uncontested market space.[1] Janice blinked and swallowed a few times as she tried to keep up with Deena.

"So, to make a long story short, there's appetite in our team to explore sustainability further. I'd like you to come back and lead the effort, not only as head of marketing but as head of strategy for us. You'll have the same compensation package you have now—I'll match it—but a much more exciting and meaningful role."

Janice felt a surge of excitement at what she was being offered. The company was in financial difficulties, with all the attendant risks of boarding a sinking ship. The money wouldn't be any better than what she was getting, and it would mean longer hours. But Janice also knew that working in this new role for a global industry leader with huge environmental and social impacts was potentially a once-in-a-lifetime opportunity to make a real difference.

Reflecting as she stirred her coffee, she thought that she would have to be sure the leadership team was truly aligned on the challenge of sustainability. To win the bet that Deena was proposing would require enormous commitment and energy from everyone. Finally, she allowed that she was inclined to accept Deena's offer but on one condition, which she proceeded to spell out.

Janice's unusual request

"I know you're anxious to get people in action and produce bottom-line results that you can take to the analysts," said Janice. "But to get the team pulling together, we'll first need to make sustainability come alive for each of them. As you know, it's got to be a whole lot more than an intellectual idea. We've got to go off-site somewhere the team can experience first-hand what's going on with society and the environment."

"Tell me a bit more what you have in mind," Deena said as she flashed back to similar points Doug has made in Yellowstone. "Because the whole leadership team has to make a choice," replied Janice. "They have to choose to look at the company's business activities from a broader perspective of impacts on human health, community well-being, and our air, soil, and water. It's not a technical decision, it's not a financial calculation—it's an emotional engagement. And you're not going to get that in a conference room.

"My condition for accepting the role you've proposed is that the leadership team goes off-site somewhere sustainability challenges can be seen, felt, touched, someplace beautiful and isolated, in the company of high-level scientists who can provide insight into what's really going on around us. And no one can bring their cellphones, computers, or pagers. Then when we return from the off-site, we'll meet in our boardroom and give everyone a choice—an informed choice. At that point if we get a consensus from everyone, it's more likely to stick."

Deena knew that this kind of off-site would provoke a lot of resistance. Roberto and Prakash would no doubt consider it a complete waste of time. Even Andy might wonder whether the company could afford a week of top-management time spent contemplating nature. She hoped it could be done quickly and efficiently, somewhere not too unpleasant—say the Caribbean for a couple of days.

But Janice had other ideas. She knew where she wanted to take the team and, just as importantly, who would be their guide. One of her colleagues on the national science committee on climate change, Jonathan Lettup, was one of the world's leading climate change scientists and a savvy business observer. His area of special interest was Greenland.

Janice quickly sketched out what the trip might involve. It would take a week of senior management time. Deena gulped, reluctantly nodding her agreement. "And one more thing," said Janice. "You'll have to invite Scott. It's vital that he gets on board too." With a groan Deena nodded assent.

The Arctic Circle

Four months later the group huddled together in a freezing wind. The ice wall towered above them, 150 feet tall, rising off the coast under a blinding blue sky. From the deck of their research vessel, built in Finland with an ice-strengthened hull, they could observe Arctic terns, snow buntings, and the occasional black-legged kittiwake.

"Temperatures in this part of the Arctic are rising twice as fast as the rest of the world." Jonathan Lettup was pointing to a huge block of ice that had split off from the glacier, now a huge iceberg. Just as he launched into a description of the conditions that were leading to melting ice the equivalent to all the ice in the Swiss Alps, another huge sheet broke off from the main wall, creating a spectacular wall of water that raced towards them. Maxine stifled a scream and ran inside. Standing in their winter parkas next to Jonathan, the rest of their little group—Scott, Deena, Janice, Andy, Roberto, and Prakash—stood frozen in awe at a sight they had heard about but never seen, holding white-knuckled onto the railing as the ship rocked violently under their feet.

"More than 105 million acres of ice have already melted in the last 15 years," Jonathan was saying. "During 2005, there was a record melt for seven days that covered all of southern Greenland. It was the largest melt area ever recorded on the ice sheet, surpassing the previous record in 2002.

"Because the island is mostly covered by ice and protrudes into the temperate latitudes, what goes on here is one of the best ways to measure climate change in the rest of the world. It's basically a warning of things to come, the canary in the coal mine. What you see here the rest of the planet will see in 15 to 20 years. At the current rate of melt, the ocean levels are expected to rise one meter—three feet—within our children's lifetimes. But no one really knows how fast Greenland's ice will disappear. It has already surprised all the leading scientists by melting at a much faster rate than predicted. If all of Greenland's ice melted, ocean levels would rise by about seven meters—that's 23 feet."

Deena asked, "Are all the world's islands equally at risk?" Jonathan replied cautiously. "Sea-level rise isn't only because of melting ice. It's also happening because of the heating of the oceans that's causing thermal expansion of the water. And, unlike what most people think, the rise in water level isn't expected to be uniform around the world. It'll depend on things like currents, winds, and tides as well as different rates of warming regionally. So it's hard to say what will happen at a specific location. But, yes, islands like Kiribati, Tuvalu, the Maldives, and the Bahamas are likely to be at risk. And actually it's not just future risk. It's already happening now. One of the most beautiful isles of Kiribati, called Deketik, is now two islands, with the ocean where land once was. Sea walls are crumbling and freshwater lagoons are dying as salt water moves in.

"And, speaking of islands, here on Greenland a new one is forming off the east coast where none existed before. The locals are calling it Uunartoq Qeqertoq, or Warming Island, a reference to the huge ice melts that are giving rise to it."

"How many people will be affected in the most likely scenario of a sea-level rise?" Scott asked from the back of the group, his voice tight with concern.

"Well, if the sea level did rise one meter, it's expected that 200 million people would be affected—not only in Bangladesh and on the Chinese coast, but also in the Netherlands, Japan, the United States and, of course, all low-lying islands. Flooding of homes, soil erosion, and the destruction of roads, factories, electric utilities, and other infrastructure are all part of the likely consequences. Financial costs would likely be in the trillions of dollars."

After this exchange the group, somewhat stunned, stood together mostly in silence, occasionally adding a layer of sun lotion or taking off an outer jacket as the afternoon sun warmed them—all of them awed by the enormity of the northern ocean.

An hour later, the ship anchored at a research station fixed to the ice sheet. "Every time I come here to visit, this station has had to be moved north," said Jonathan.

As the group stepped gingerly onto the glacier's surface, Jonathan pointed to what looked like fissures and crevices breaking through the ice. Asked what caused this, Jonathan explained, "This is ice flow from where you have so much tension in the ice that it cannot stick together. It breaks and opens a crevice which can go all the way down, lubricating the bottom of the ice sheet and helping it move off the bedrock and out to sea." The group could hear the water running fast and deep.

A little bit further on and much to his delight, Andy was the first to spot a polar bear, sunning itself on the glacier's western edge. The whole group had read up on the polar bear, learning that it can only hunt on ice, that the long coarse hairs of its fur were hollow and transparent, helping to keep it buoyant in the water, and that the name "Arctic" comes from ancient Greek meaning "Land of the Great Bear." Soon everyone's cameras were out and clicking.

Jonathan told them that, because the ice is breaking up earlier in the year, he was now finding female bears 55 pounds lighter than had been the case 20 years ago—frailer mothers with fewer cubs. Broken, floating chunks of ice were causing bears to weaken from hunger and, in some cases, drown. The US Fish and Wildlife Service is studying whether the polar bear should be listed as a species threatened with extinction because of the potential loss of the summer ice cap.

"The bears are unlikely to survive as a species if there's a complete loss of ice in summer," said Jonathan, "which could happen by the end of this century." Of course, there are skeptics who question climate change projections like that, saying they're no more reliable than your local weatherman. But Jonathan insisted that arctic projections were proving accurate and, if anything, too conservative. "That said, the skeptics have brought up some very interesting issues over the last few years. And they've forced us to think more and more about the data that we collect. We owe the skeptics a vote of thanks for making our science as precise as it is today."

Toxic complications

As Deena's team watched in awe, their bear suddenly snapped upright, deftly catching an unsuspecting ringed seal that had come up for air at a hole in the ice. "That's the polar bear's main food source," explained Jonathan. "If they can't find enough seal, they will eat walrus, young beluga whale, narwhal, fish, and even seabirds and their eggs.

"At the top of the food chain, with such a fatty diet, polar bears are also threatened by persistent organic pollutants (POPs) including a wide range of poisonous substances that stay in the environment for a long time. These substances become concentrated in parts of the Arctic, owing to the direction of prevailing winds and ocean currents."

"We've all got some knowledge of chemistry given the industry we're in," said Roberto. "What kind of poisonous substances are we talking about?" Everyone in the group knew Roberto was challenging Jonathan, waiting to poke holes in what he still saw as an environmentalist sob story.

Jonathan rattled off a list of chemicals the group knew were particularly nasty: "Organochlorines, of which many are polychlorinated biphenyls (PCBs), dichlorodiphenyl trichloroethane (also known as DDT), its metabolites, chlordanes, dieldrin, hexacyclohexanes, hexachlorobenzene, and polybrominated diphenyl ethers (PBDEs)."

"And how do we know the concentration levels of these chemicals are enough to cause damage in polar bears? Trace amounts might not mean much," persisted Roberto.

"Well, let me put it to you this way," said Jonathan with a chuckle. "The ice cap isn't the only thing shrinking in the Arctic. Recent studies show that the genitals of polar bears in Greenland are apparently dwindling in size because of industrial pollutants. In the worst case, it could endanger the bears by spoiling their love lives and causing their numbers to decline."

Janice added her own observations: "Bears with high levels of POPs also have low levels of vitamin A, thyroid hormones, and some antibodies—all of which are important for their normal development and ability to fight off diseases. Organochlorine exposure also leads to disruptions in their bone mineral composition. All marine mammals in the Arctic are being affected by these pollutants. Polar bears and other large marine mammals such as killer whales and pilot whales now carry extremely high levels of these contaminants."

Roberto was silent as he stared at the solitary bear working its way through its meal.

"In fact, polar bears here are among the most polluted animals in the wild, the blubber of the seals they feast on having accumulated high levels of the toxic substances. And, as you might know, Roberto, organohalogens can act like hormones, which is what we believe is leading to the shrinkage in their testes."

As they talked back and forth, they could plainly see plastic trash—lots of it—bobbing into view on the ocean's surface not far from the ship. Pointing to the flotsam, Jonathan explained that plastic trash dumped in the ocean is often swept to shore, but much is trapped by calm winds and sluggish water within the ocean's loop of currents. Plastic debris—everything from Japanese traffic cones to canisters of American motor oil—breaks down into smaller pieces that act as a sponge for toxic chemicals, soaking up a million-fold greater concentration of such deadly compounds as PCBs than the surrounding sea water. That could turn a bellyful of plastic in a polar bear from a mere stomach ache to a toxic gut bomb. In some parts of the Northern Pacific ocean, plastic reaches concentrations of over a million pieces per square mile—more plastic than plankton!

The raw beauty of the north suddenly began to take on a different quality. Their mood became somber as the afternoon sun lowered into the horizon. Janice felt the trip was accomplishing at least some of her goals for the group.

The next day they were set to fly back from Kangerlussuaq to Chicago via Baltimore. That last evening on the ship, they had a feast of fish, squid, seal, and other raw delicacies. Their Russian captain joined them with a bottle of ice-cold Koskenkorva, the strong Finnish vodka, which after a week of water and flat colas was a hugely welcome change of pace. Soon Russian songs were playing loudly on the ship's intercom system, Prakash and Andy were singing ribald songs, and Maxine was dancing with the captain to everyone's noisy clapping. Scott and Deena, seated diagonally across from each other, were trying to chat above the noise and occasionally just being contemplative under the black night sky.

The team chooses

The following Monday back at the office, Deena held her usual staff meeting. This time it was also attended by Scott Giffen. In spite of his presence, a mood of congeniality prevailed as Deena asked each person to share insights from their trip. The commentary was equal parts about their bonding as a team, individual reflections on the northern icescape, and dismay at what they learned about climate change and the decline of the Arctic.

Scott had perhaps the biggest insight of all. "Somehow we're part of the system that's causing global climate change, that's creating an environment toxic to marine mammals, and that's allowing plastic bags to float up to Baffin Bay. We may not be directly responsible but, as the saying goes, if you're not a part of the solution, you're a part of the problem." To which Deena added, "With a price–earnings ratio stuck around eight, we're not creating much value for our shareholders either."

Somewhat awkwardly, Janice tried to jump into the silence that followed: "So, do we make sustainability a key priority in our core business, or not?"

But Deena wasn't quite ready yet and, more importantly, she sensed that the others weren't either. While everyone seemed further along in their thinking after their week in the Arctic, they weren't ready yet to commit to something they couldn't fully comprehend. "I'm not convinced," she said simply. "But I'm willing to consider it. Personally, I'd like to first know our environmental and social footprint, and compare it with what we think our company would look like if we were sustainable and profitable."

Everyone in the team agreed that it made sense to take a closer look. From their reactions Deena could tell the team wanted to move ahead with sustainability, but that there was still some fear that it wouldn't be a sound business decision. In essence, by expressing a conditional desire to take a closer look, she had smartly got them to buy in without having to commit outright.

Scott Giffen stood up to leave. "I expect this team to come up with a breakthrough, not only for this business unit and for our company as a whole. I'd like to see us reassert leadership in our industry.

"Just remember," he added as he closed his briefcase. "While it's a great feeling to do the right thing, to know that you are going to make the world a better place, you can't lose sight of business priorities—getting productivity and profit margins back on track, improving our brand image with customers, growing our market share, and bringing in new talent at every level of the organization."

"Which means," added Deena, "that sustainability can't come at an overall cost to our business. The game has to be about elevating value to our shareholders and to our stakeholders. No one is allowed to come back to Scott or the Board with compromises." She smiled brightly as she looked around the room.

After he left, the group spent half an hour planning next steps, discussing who needed to be on what teams, and scheduling a meeting for the next decision point.

Outside assistance

That afternoon, Deena and Janice called the consultants who had helped Doug's company. With their help, they would get the expertise they needed to do the footprint analysis and visioning of a corporate future that would be worth investing in.

After a first meeting and to Deena's surprise, one of the lead consultants put them in touch with more than a dozen other organizations. "We don't have the expertise to do everything ourselves," he said, "but we can help coordinate the job."

To carry out the footprint analysis, the consultants brought in leading environmental NGOs such as ProtectEarth. They also called on Human Rights Assurance International and a few fairtrade NGOs. To Deena's surprise, experts from each of these organizations worked easily with her team and spent almost no time criticizing or preaching an activist agenda.

Within three weeks, they had a broad life-cycle assessment of their business unit's major environmental and social impacts. For each of their facilities and products, they could see clearly their greenhouse gas emissions, energy use, water consumption, airborne carcinogens, soil toxicity, and hazardous chemicals use. For each of their major supply chains, they saw their exposures in terms of fair wages, diversity, and human rights risks.

What made the footprint reports so powerful were the diverse perspectives given by the consultants, experts, and NGOs. Each impact was benchmarked according to industry best practices and related to the major sustainability challenges facing the planet.

"What makes the sustainability footprint valuable to me," Roberto was saying to Janice, "is that the environmental problems we saw in the Arctic are clearly linked to the environmental impacts of our business. And it goes a step further to show the business risks of continuing with our current negative impacts and the business opportunities of making a change."

Janice beamed. "I hear your operations team has an early win?"

"We sure do," replied Roberto. "One of our big sellers to the abrasives industry is a specialty coating with a synthetic blue dye. By changing the intensity of the blue by one degree, we cut our negative environmental impact by 50%. Not only do our customers not notice the difference in technical performance, they actually prefer a dye that they can tout as environmentally friendly to their customers. Our orders are up 15% for next month."

Janice couldn't help be amazed how Roberto, one of the biggest critics of pursuing a sustainability strategy, was now in action and producing tangible results.

Joining them around the coffee machine was Art, who felt both vindicated and frustrated by the team's response. "We've already had much of this data internally," he pointed out. "It's in our EH&S reports and in the notes to the CSR report." Roberto looked at him deadpan and asked, "What's a CSR report?" Janice stepped in between them before things got ugly.

But they both had a point. The information already existed in the company, yet no one had bothered to look at it—until now, when top management made it a strategic priority and external consultants were brought in to treat it.

Whole-system change

In a planning meeting the following week, Deena and Janice agreed to hold a strategy summit six months down the road to brainstorm what a sustainable and profitable future for the company would look like. What would make it different from other strategy summits was their plan to invite front-line employees, customers, suppliers, environmental organizations, social NGOs, academics, and policy experts—over 800 people in all.

Janice proposed that they use a whole-system approach to organizational change. The usual reductive problem-solving in small insular groups wouldn't be as effective. Janice said she had already experienced the power of a whole-system change methodology called Appreciative Inquiry, and recommended it strongly to Deena.

"Tell me about Appreciative Inquiry," Deena asked Janice.

"Instead of getting change to happen in small groups of eight to ten people at a time, it's a way to engage large groups of people to represent all parts of a whole system. It's a systems approach to change—perfect for when you're dealing with complex issues involving lots of different stakeholders." Janice paused before continuing. "By using a whole-system approach, we can get a clearer picture of how our business creates, or destroys, value for our stakeholders. Instead of the usual corporate thinking about environmental and social issues, it'll give us an opportunity to listen for an outside perspective. Of course, we need to be smart about who we invite. We don't have to include activists who want only to harm us, or groups with political agendas. The goal should be to get a cross-section of everyone who cares about and has a stake in the future of our business.

"But there is another key advantage to Appreciative Inquiry—AI for short—in addition to the whole-system approach," she continued. "It uses a positive 'lens' to consider change not from the perspective of what is wrong with an organization, but from its core strengths. The vision of a sustainable company needs to be positive and life-affirming. A strength-based approach allows participants to discover the best of their shared experiences, and to tap into the larger system's capacity for cooperation."

Deena was feeling a little nervous at the prospect of a "life-affirming" meeting with 800 people including customers and critics, but she instinctively trusted Janice. The trip to the Arctic had also left her and the senior management team more open to talking about these kinds of issues.

"We'll need to invite employees from across our organization. Dispatch clerks, fork-lift operators, marketing assistants, as well as country managers, and your own staff," continued Janice. "When we 'dream' a future that is both profitable and good for the world, we'll be doing it with everyone involved. That's going to allow us to go much faster than if we held only small group meetings and then sent memos out to everyone explaining the new vision."

Deena looked a little worried. "I hope this isn't going to be everyone getting together to sing 'Kumbaya.' How is that going to mesh with our message that our business is facing critical pressures and we need to produce bottom-line results now?"

Janice cut in. "AI summits are totally task-focused. Yes, we'll design it to build a shared vision, but our ultimate goal at the summit will be to get momentum for our business priorities. The intention is for us to walk away with a clear plan of action for becoming a sustainable company in ways that benefit the business and society."

Deena still looked a little skeptical with her forehead furrowed in concern, but decided it was worth the gamble.

The strategy summit

The first thing Deena and Janice did was to set up a highly diverse and representative steering committee to prepare the strategy summit. In addition to the two of them, the only other member of top management was Andy, the CFO. Other steering committee members included plant managers, sales reps, laboratory technicians, and several front-line employees—a total of 25 in all from various product areas and manufacturing sites.

The steering committee put a great deal of effort into defining the task of the strategy summit: the purpose behind the work that the organization was about to undertake. The steering committee then gathered for an off-site meeting to learn about sustainability and what other companies are doing about it as well as to get a taste for Appreciative Inquiry. During the meeting the group decided on who should be invited.

Five months later, over 800 people including employees, customers, suppliers, and NGOs gathered for the summit. Deena opened it by addressing everyone in the huge convention center selected for the occasion. She began by encouraging everyone to "come together with an open mind and to contribute new ideas that will help us all—each and every-one of us—to achieve what we are personally committed to *and* what makes smart business sense so that we, as a company, can be around to help those ideas become a reality." Roberto leaned over to Prakash and remarked that this didn't sound much like the Deena they had known in past years.

In small groups of 10 to 15 people sitting at round tables spread through-out the huge hall, the collective group got down to business, beginning with a set of questions to uncover the greatest aspects of the company and to create a shared vision of a more sustainable future for everyone. They discussed ways that the company could adopt sustainability in its day-to-day business practices without sacrificing any of the organization's core positive elements.

One of the exercises produced the following list of key features which the working group believed the company would have once it became a truly sustainable company:

- Sustainability performance is fully integrated into the strategy of the company

- All managers consider sustainability to be part of their daily job

- Metrics reward managers for sustainability performance

- The CEO and senior leadership demonstrate full support and "walk the talk"

- Sustainability targets are set and progress monitored. They are detailed and quantitative

- New management tools are used including stakeholder engage-ment, environmental accounting, design for environment (DfE), life-cycle assessment (LCA), product declarations, balanced score-cards, and sustainability due diligence

- Broad and diverse relationships exist between the company and outside stakeholders, including partnerships with NGOs or other organizations previously considered fringe or adversarial to the business

- Managers are able to uncover business innovations that fully integrate environmental and social dimension in their core lines of business

- New elements of corporate culture are added to the legacy culture—greater accountability and transparency as well as the ability to listen and to empathize with diverse points of view

These and other ideas were presented, discussed, and widely shared throughout the full group.

The large-scale brainstorming session gave way to a selection process that focused on choosing action initiatives that captured smart business ideas along with the excitement of the participants. Ultimately, 15 initiatives were retained and participants chose which ones they wanted to work on based upon expertise and motivation. The initiatives ranged from redesigning the mission and principles of the organization to include the environmental and social dimensions, to new bio-based products with more sustainable packaging and transportation methods.

Regardless of the focus of the initiative, each team was challenged to come up with a clear description of what it entailed, how it would benefit the organization, and a plan for implementation. This provided consistency and validation for each of the projects, allowing everyone to leave with specific action items to work on and a plan for execution.

Walking between the groups in animated discussion around the tables, Deena found the level of energy and richness of ideas absolutely awe-inspiring. "No one would have believed that 15 sustainable value initiatives could be put together in just a few days," she commented to Janice.

As the summit drew to an end, there was a growing sense of enthusiasm about the future, the direction in which the organization was heading, and the determination to get there. And it was not just the employees who felt positive and encouraged. Many of the formerly critical external stakeholders who participated in the summit shared the enthusiasm. Michael Reinford, one of the invited NGOs, expressed his views on the outcomes of the summit. "The end result is a whole-system vision for positive social change to reduce greenhouse gases and reduce energy use—perhaps even make some of the company's manufacturing sites net exporters of energy—to shift the company's portfolio to eco-friendly products that actually benefit the Earth, and to create new cooperative relationships with partners along the supply chain. These are lofty goals which will require constant, determined effort by everyone in the company if they are to be met. Do I think they will be met? After this dialog with the company and its partners, not only do I think the company can do it, I know that it will."

The sustainable company

The summit produced a profound transformation in the level of engage-ment and alignment both inside and outside of the company. Not every-one agreed with the outcome of the working groups, and several vocal critics remained but, by and large, the water-cooler conversations shifted from dwelling on what was wrong with the organization to a new sense of excitement about the future. There was a feeling that the 15 action ini-tiatives held a huge promise for the company and its partners.

The guiding vision was of a new kind of company that makes profits while no longer relying on fossil fuels such as coal and oil, reducing its energy costs *and* its future greenhouse gas emission liabilities. It was about achieving zero waste at every stage from raw materials to product packaging and disposal—saving the expense of paying someone to make the waste in the first place, and then paying someone else to haul it away. It was about non-toxic product parts and manufacturing by-products that are either biodegradable (they decompose and become food in nature's cycle) or they can be recycled again and again. Such a company's footprint is close to zero—taking nothing from the Earth that is not renewable, and doing no harm to people or planet. It may even have a "negative foot-print" as it provides environmental and social solutions to others: for example, working with suppliers on fairtrade contracts or with client companies to offer them clean energy systems. The company becomes restorative—putting back on balance more than it takes from the Earth, and doing good for society. The employees of such a company are greatly energized as a result of the strategy, feeling as never before that through their jobs they are able to make a positive contribution to the world they live in. Best of all, such a company is poised for huge growth and prof-itability as it meets the surging demand for market-based solutions to the world's growing environmental and social challenges.

Sustainable value networks

In the first few months after the summit, bottom-line results were yet to be achieved. Teams called Sustainable Value Networks (SV Networks) were formed with business managers and outside stakeholders working in close partnership on one or more of the 15 initiatives. "Quick wins" were given priority to gain momentum.

The SV Networks were responsible for identifying which key external stakeholders to involve in the initiatives, from customers and suppliers to NGOs, local communities, and technical experts. Value was placed on those individuals and organizations that thought differently about the issues being addressed, and who were willing to be constructive in how to tackle solutions. Line managers (those with profit and loss responsibility for the business units involved) were appointed to drive the overall work of the networks. They set business targets and developed quantitative indicators of performance. They aligned on the principles and values that would guide their action. Their leaders worked hard to make sure that people understood that the SV Networks were about advancing business priorities and not "saving the whales" (as important, of course, as that may be).

Value was placed on creativity and on the variety of solutions: for example, not only energy efficiency and waste reduction but also sustainable products and new markets to address unmet societal needs.

The SV Networks soon realized that innovations could come from anywhere and from all levels of the organization. New tools and approaches were adopted including systematic stakeholder engagement and product stewardship that tracked volatile organic compounds (VOCs), hazardous air pollutants (HAPs), water use, waste, and emissions of nitrous oxide and greenhouse gases. Management systems introduced sustainability accounting and reporting, DfE with LCA and product declarations, cradle-to-cradle (C2C) design criteria for products and processes, and ISO 14001—to name just a few.

Deena and her top-management team made it a priority to reward the SV Networks, as well as the individual managers and external stakeholders involved, for sustainable value performance. The senior management team also actively reinforced new elements of corporate culture such as a greater willingness to take risks and to learn from mistakes. New organizational competencies were developed through training and education programs for the top 1,000 managers worldwide.

Deena's team pushed hard to encourage collaboration across functions. For example, product designers and buyers were required to work with plant managers assisted by outside NGOs with specific sustainability know-how.

Sustainable value results

One year later, the first low-hanging fruit began producing financial results—and the numbers were astonishing. According to Andy, the sustainability initiatives in the first year had contributed over $500 million to the bottom line. Highly visible projects[2] put the company back on a track of growth and profitability, the result of the company's new strategy to focus on sustainable value—value that is positive for shareholders *and* stakeholders. The projects provided practical and specific evidence that sustainability was a source of competitive advantage for the company. In many cases, sustainability pressures created unheard-of breakthroughs that no one would have believed in the business-as-usual context that had existed until recently.

A case in point: the energy SV Network designed a new manufacturing facility that operated at the same production rates producing the same products as a conventionally designed facility, but that consumed *90% less energy*. Working with NGOs specialized in energy efficiency and resource productivity, the team used whole-system optimization to design the new production line. This led to radical changes:

- Big pipes and small motors to pump the viscous liquids instead of small pipes and big motors

- A production line that was installed around big straight pipes rather than installing the production line first and then bending the pipes here and there to fit them to the line

The result was a production facility that cost less to build and less to operate than its conventionally designed counterpart of equal capacity.

The same energy SV Network designed a manufacturing facility near a city with an unregulated landfill and, in partnership with the city, committed $5 million in capital costs to capture and pipe the methane from the landfill to the factory nine miles away. The factory spent $100,000 to adapt four boilers, representing 40% of the factory's total energy usage, to substitute the methane for the fossil fuel currently used. The price of the captured methane is 30% less than the fossil fuel. Calculations show that the landfill will have a life of 40 years, which translates into a net present value (NPV) of over $50 million for the city. The company reduced its energy costs by 12% and, because methane has a global warming potential (GWP) that is 23 times as much as carbon dioxide, the factory receives a further benefit of a greenhouse gas offset of $23 \times 40\% = 920\%$ of its total energy consumption. And, of course, the Earth is spared the greenhouse gas emissions.

The recover/recycle/re-use SV Network worked on the re-use of plastic polymers that typically end up in landfills. In the past, recycled plastics amounted to less than 5% of inputs to the manufacturing process. After just six months of working on new process innovations to re-use plastics, the division was able to re-use over 30% of recycled product as raw material input.

Several SV Networks were dedicated to sustainable products and markets. New plant-based polymers were developed to replace polyethylene and polypropylene plastics. Biodegradable coatings that could be manufactured and sold to low-income populations in countries such as China and India helped generate jobs and economic growth in rural areas. New membrane components were developed for fuel cell technologies and high-performance polymer tips for windmills—small, yet fast-growing, markets in the carbon-constrained world of tomorrow.

Janice and her Sales & Marketing team spent much of their time on consumer education and awareness for sustainability products that offered the win–win of better business performance and greater benefits for society. Roberto in operations worked with suppliers to share his team's knowledge of energy effectiveness and reduced materials intensity—in some cases even selling this knowledge to suppliers through consulting services.

Another SV Network focused on health, wellness, and safety in order to reduce health costs for the company. After several hundred employees took part in a six-month health program, 180 achieved lower cholesterol levels, 100 reduced their blood pressure, and 140 reduced their blood sugar levels. The initiative led to measurable increases in productivity, and reduced absenteeism and employee turnover.

The company's culture and leadership style remained no-nonsense and results-oriented; ideas for saving the world that required trade-offs for consumers, or lost money for the company, were rejected. But these remained surprisingly rare as the new sustainability strategy permeated the organization—a snowball effect in evidence as creativity and breakthrough thinking, fueled by a deep sense of purpose, led to success after success. Earnings-per-share rose steadily from that point onwards.

A surprise visit

Eighteen months after the strategy summit, Deena was hard at work crafting her presentation for the Annual Shareholders' Meeting, during which she would share the company's business and financial performance for the year, when her assistant walked in to announce a surprise visitor. Michael Reinford, her critic a few years back, was in Chicago with two chief executives who wanted to meet her.

In a short hand-written note brought in by her assistant, he had written: "Would be delighted if you could meet with us—my guests would like to see what authenticity, integrity, and coherence mean in business." Deena smiled to herself. This year would be a banner year for her unit: record profits and growth. Agencies that rated social investment had ranked her company among the top three in the industry, while her team was motivated as never before and, on a personal level, her work had taken on once again huge meaning.

Business had never been so good.

Part II
Mainstream companies that are doing well by doing good

Every single pressing social and global issue of our time is a business opportunity.

Peter Drucker, author, teacher, and consultant

A growing number of global industry leaders are adopting sustainability strategies in their core business. These include DuPont, Wal-Mart, Lafarge, Cargill's NatureWorks, Novo Nordisk, Marks & Spencer, Toyota, General Electric, Unilever, Danone, Alcoa, Philips, JP Morgan Chase, and many others. Because of their size and complexity these companies inevitably attract critics and none can be deemed sustainable everywhere all the time. However, perfection shouldn't get in the way of the good; the fact that these companies are consciously integrating the environmental and social dimensions into their core business—not only to reduce harm but also in an effort to profit from doing good—is a signal that something profound is going on in the game of capitalism.

The four case studies in Part II have been chosen to illustrate the central theme that companies can create value for their shareholders and stakeholders in a classic win–win situation. Each case study is of a mainstream corporation (not a specialty player in a green niche) that sought to create value for its shareholders by integrating sustainability into its core business. The case studies are structured to allow the reader to easily understand the environmental or social challenge being addressed by each company, and how their solutions created business value in addition to societal value. The final section of each case study provides insights into the organizational journey the company took:

- Who championed the case
- How the decision was made to invest resources in it
- What relationships contributed to its execution

The four case studies tell the real-life stories of a handful of pioneering companies that have managed to integrate sustainability into the fabric of their businesses—and are better off as a result.

4

The new competitive environment

A positive outlook on business and society is more than just "feel good" wishful thinking. Mainstream publicly traded companies are now able to play a leading role in solving the world's toughest problems because a new competitive environment has emerged. Pressing ecological and social challenges have become big business opportunities. "Sustainability-as-business-opportunity" is now shifting from the domain of niche players to global industry leaders, from Stonyfield Farms to Danone, from Patagonia to Wal-Mart, and from The Co-operative Bank to JP Morgan Chase. Three of the four case studies from my last book, *The Sustainable Company*, were about mid-size companies with partially non-public ownership. Three of the four cases in *Sustainable Value* are global industry leaders with publicly traded shares.

One hundred years ago, IBM founder Thomas J. Watson Sr imagined business as "knitting together the whole fabric of civilization."[1] Today it has the global reach and market power to tackle complex challenges like climate change and to deliver timely solutions that will allow it to regain its place as an agent of world benefit. By comparison, national governments are parochial institutions with limited powers to affect change.

The question is whether global corporations will act in time to offer business solutions to global problems, or whether their executives will remain mostly reactive and defensive about their role in society. Will business leaders seek only to reduce harm when forced to by regulation and shame? Or will they grasp the growing business opportunity to do well—indeed, to do better—by doing good?

The new face of business

Suggesting that mainstream business can be an agent of world benefit invites disbelief. Against the backdrop of Friedman's injunction that the only social responsibility of business is to increase its profits, corporate malfeasance from Enron to Exxon has etched its negative image indelibly onto the public imagination.

And yet what other institution is capable of so rapidly and effectively satisfying new needs? Who else has the resources, global span, and nimbleness to turn on a dime when an opportunity presents itself? Now that the demand is growing everywhere for solutions to environmental and social problems—a marketplace demand that is not only for more widgets, but also for a healthier and more sustainable world—corporations can become good citizens and make a profit doing so.

A disconnect arises only when environmentalists and business critics attempt to force companies into roles they were never intended to play. Corporations are blamed for not being altruistic enough and for not being motivated by moral reason. They are asked to do things that benefit society at an unacceptable cost to shareholders. Asking Wal-Mart to raise wages by $3/hour is misunderstanding what it takes to compete on low margins with a workforce of nearly two million employees. Expecting oil and gas companies to instantly switch to renewable energy or car companies to adopt clean energy drivetrains before these technologies have become economically viable is simply not realistic. Pushed by tougher regulations and vocal critics in the public health community, McDonald's has added healthy salads, no-egg breakfasts, and "no-fat-no-cholesterol" bran muffins to its menu along with low-fat frozen yogurt and sorbet. But, as long as consumers continue to demand burgers and fries, the company will continue to offer its traditional fare, albeit with reduced levels of trans-fats and with nutritional facts on the wrapping.

Rather than condemn business as overly self-interested, critics would do better to understand it and harness its strength for good. The game of business is making money for shareholders. Over time, mainstream corporations will pursue sustainability performance when it advances their business priorities.

Which raises the question: how has the world changed to make sustainability a source of competitive advantage? Why are environmental and social issues increasingly driving business performance?

The new competitive environment

Five interrelated mega-trends are expanding the scope of what it means to create business value from a narrow shareholder focus to one that includes stakeholder value based on the economic, environmental, and social impacts a company has on its diverse constituents. Taken together, these trends are transforming the business landscape.

1. **There is a large and growing gap between the needs of society and what the public sector can deliver as solutions.** Governments and non-profit organizations are proving ineffective in addressing climate change, poverty, pollution, disease, and social exclusion. This gap creates an unprecedented opportunity for business to enter into collaborative partnerships with these institutions to tackle complex problems[2]

2. **Civil society is experiencing rising expectations of business in terms of health, safety, social well-being, and the environment.** For example, in many sectors increased energy efficiency is no longer enough; reducing carbon emissions to mitigate climate change is now entering mainstream consumer expectations

3. **The Internet and its low-cost collaborative platforms have enabled stakeholders to band together into self-organizing virtual communities to target corporations.** With lightning speed and across geographic boundaries, these communities of interest reward corporations that are seen as advancing their interests and penalize those who are not.[3] Recent tactics include using Hollywood documentaries, *YouTube* videos and Google maps

to spread messages to a new audience about perceived undesirable business practices[4]

4. **New market mechanisms attach a price to environmental and social impacts.** For example, the London and Chicago Climate Exchanges now provide a way for companies to financially value reductions in greenhouse gas emissions. Meanwhile, the growth in "green" investors is raising the cost of capital for companies that are seen as worse than their peers in terms of non-renewable energy use or human rights violations

5. **New legislation is adding tougher performance standards and new levels of complexity to business in a broad range of sectors.** California's AB32, a bill signed into law by Governor Schwarzenegger in September 2006, mandates a 25% reduction in carbon dioxide emissions by 2020. The European Union's Registration, Evaluation, and Authorization of Chemicals (REACH) Regulation requires companies to disclose the composition and human health impact of chemicals found in their products. Both pieces of legislation require companies in a range of sectors to invest in higher environmental performance standards

Together, these five mega-trends are giving stakeholders a new-found power to effect corporate change.[5] A committed cadre is willing to act against companies that fail to meet new societal expectations and reward those who do.[6] At the forefront are international NGOs, which have grown in number from a few thousand in 1970 to over 60,000 today. There are also an estimated 3–4 million "mom-and-pop" NGOs and over 100 million bloggers as of late 2007. With their unique ability to mobilize public opinion, NGOs at times coalesce with activist shareholders, governments, consumers, and the media to create a "perfect storm" of pressures on business. The stakeholder value created or destroyed by a company has now become an important business issue in addition to a moral one.

The new competitive environment does not make business single-handedly responsible for solving global problems. Business cannot be expected to come up with solutions entirely on its own. Climate change and global poverty, to name only two global issues, will require cooperation and co-leadership with government and civil society. Also important will be consumer awareness of global issues and of how their choices contribute to a healthier and more sustainable future. Collaboration is vital to solving complex problems involving multiple stakeholders, both

in terms of the knowledge required and the alignment of key relationships.

As the case examples suggest and, as described further in Part III, the
new competitive environment will require managers to adopt a different
leadership mind-set and a more disciplined approach to integrating
stakeholder value in their organizations. To take advantage of sustainability-related business opportunities, managers will have to learn to see
their value chains as whole systems in which multiple stakeholders co-
innovate sustainable value solutions.

The time is now

Many of us have the uneasy feeling that we will soon, collectively, come
to a fork in the road: we will *either* become irreversibly embroiled in costly
wars with widespread environmental damage and increasingly militant
groups of the socially excluded poor *or* we will shift human consciousness
and combine political will with technological ingenuity to create a
healthier and more prosperous future for all.

Arguments are persuasive for both scenarios: terrorism and environmental damage are worsening, yet heroes from the business world are
making remarkable strides in tackling global challenges. Mohammed
Yunus, Bill Gates, Warren Buffet, and Richard Branson are helping to
address problems from Aids and global poverty to climate change. Global
industry CEOs such as Patrick Cescau of Unilever, Chad Holliday of
DuPont, Katsuaki Watanabe at Toyota, and Lee Scott at Wal-Mart are
pushing socially responsible and eco-friendly business practices into
mainstream markets.

Let's assume for a moment that the turning point is in as little as the
next ten years. We are confronted with the need to make the transition
from an industrial growth society that exploits people and nature, to a
life-sustaining society. If we fail, we will muddle along in a period of pro-
tracted decline with unstable markets and economic depression leading
to even more social and environmental chaos.

Who will lead the way forward? What institution or organization?

An underlying "big idea" in this book is that corporations, as the most
powerful and global form of organization on Earth, are uniquely suited to
providing innovative solutions to seemingly intractable social and environmental challenges. Without them, the world faces the truly Sysiphean

task of trying to solve deep, systemic, global challenges with outdated national (or multinational but still not truly global) institutions capable of only piecemeal policies.

Where social responsibility and profits converge

In the past, managers often felt forced to choose between two perspectives: business has a moral responsibility to society *or* it has a fiduciary responsibility to its shareholders. Those who believe in the profit motive consider moral questions in the workplace to be a distraction. Those who believe in a societal role for business consider the single-minded focus on short-term profits to be irresponsible.

In the new global business environment, companies can pursue both simultaneously. Indeed, they must if they want to succeed. Companies that deliver profits to shareholders while destroying value for society are incurring hidden liabilities. Those that offer *solutions* to environmental and social challenges are discovering huge profit opportunities. The corporate path to doing well by doing good has become the smart way to do business—if you have the knowledge and competencies required for it.

5
DuPont

Now we see ourselves in a third phase of sustainable growth, characterized by a holistic approach that is fully integrated into our business models. In this phase, sustainability is broadened to include human safety as well as environmental protection, and it becomes our market-driven business priority throughout the value chain . . . For us, sustainability is not just a corporate mission; it is also a business imperative for success in the 21st century.

Chad Holliday, CEO, DuPont

Company overview

DuPont, a $27 billion company with 60,000 employees, began life in 1802 manufacturing gunpowder and explosives. Since then it has reinvented itself many times—first by moving into dyes, resins, and paints in the early 20th century and later becoming an energy company with its acquisition of Conoco in 1983. Still the second largest chemical manufacturer in the US, it redefined itself once more in the early 1990s as "the world's most dynamic science company, creating sustainable solutions essential to a better, safer and healthier life for people everywhere." The question many observers will ask about this latest rebirth is: Hype or a real change in business strategy?

DuPont is now pursuing business opportunities in agriculture, nutrition, and bio-based materials while shifting away from its traditional lower-growth businesses that rely heavily on fossil fuels. The shift is evident in its sale of the Dacron®, Lycra®, and Nylon® divisions and the creation of The Solae Company (soy foods) and Pioneer Hi-bred International, Inc. (bio-tech seeds) businesses.

Many of DuPont's sustainable value initiatives since 1991 have focused on climate change action, which makes it particularly relevant as a case study at a time when climate change is becoming a significant sustainability issue—and one that is rising fast on the public agenda.

DuPont is a member of the US Climate Action Partnership, a group of originally ten companies and four NGOs (including Alcoa, GE, and BP America) which in early 2007 began urging President Bush to support mandatory reductions in greenhouse gas (GHG) emissions and to propose federal reduction targets.

DuPont as villain

While DuPont's share price rose steadily during much of the 1990s, the company was garnering unwanted attention from environmental watchdogs, public-interest groups, and government regulators. Among its dubious distinctions during the decade, DuPont was nominated to the following "worst of" lists:

- "Shameless: 1995's ten worst corporations" by *Multinational Monitor*

- "1999 Dirty Five," one of the five biggest polluters in the US by the Public Interest Research Group (PIRG)

- "Top US polluter of 1995" by the US Environmental Protection Agency (EPA)

- "Least-wanted companies 1993" by the Council on Economic Priorities

According to the current CEO Chad Holliday, DuPont began to mobilize its sustainability efforts in earnest in 1988 after Greenpeace activists scaled the wall of one of its plants and hung a giant banner "DuPont Number 1 Polluter" facing a highway used by thousands of commuters. Holliday recalls that event as the spark that led the company to clean up its act. The fear of being singled out as one of the world's top corporate villains continued to motivate the company's top management during much of the 1990s.

According to Dr Paul Tebo, the company's corporate vice president for health, safety, and the environment between 1993 and 2004, the initial foray into sustainability was also motivated by a desire to get ahead of the curve on government regulation. A science-based corporate culture forced top management to take seriously the link between greenhouse gas emissions and climate change, much as science had made the case to the international community for phasing out chlorofluorocarbons (CFCs) in the previous two decades. DuPont was the first company to announce a phase-out of CFCs and the first to develop and commercialize CFC alternatives—particularly for refrigeration and air conditioning, which represented about 60% of CFC use worldwide. Its profitable leadership in phasing in CFC alternatives helped demonstrate to management the business benefits of a first-move advantage based on good science.

DuPont's greenhouse gas emissions problem

In 1990 DuPont was a major producer of nitrous oxides (N_2O) and fluorocarbons such as HFC-23, a by-product of HCFC-22 manufacture. These gases have a global warming potential of 310 times and 11,700 times that of carbon dioxide (CO_2), respectively. By 1991, DuPont's own atmospheric scientists were beginning to sound the alarm bell about the company's emissions and what they might mean down the road for climate change and impending regulation. As Paul Tebo says:

> DuPont made its first commitment to greenhouse gas reductions in 1991 based on information from our atmospheric scientists that the link with climate change was sufficiently clear that responsible actions should be taken. The majority of the emission reductions in the 1990s was in non-CO_2 gases and cost the company money.[1]

At the time, there was little sense of opportunity for competitive advantage other than anticipating government regulations. Nevertheless, the early experience in emission reductions had two important business benefits:

- It helped fuel energy conservation including a search for less energy-intensive products and processes
- It gave DuPont valuable insights into emissions trading

Ultimately, the initial reductions in greenhouse gas emissions were also to lay the foundation for a holistic sustainability strategy that would extend up and down the company's value chain and fundamentally restructure its product portfolio.

Business opportunities in a carbon-constrained world

Energy conservation and emission reductions led to $3 billion in avoided costs between 1991 and 2005. To illustrate the energy conservation efforts, in some cases DuPont replaced fossil fuels such as natural gas with methane from landfills in its industrial boilers while, in other cases, it redesigned industrial processes to squeeze efficiencies from its chemicals manufacturing. Overall the company managed to reduce global energy use by 7% below 1990 levels, exceeding early on its goal of holding energy use flat through 2010.

Emissions reductions eventually made money for the company. The sale of emission reduction credits on the London Climate Exchange, based on efforts by UK facilities, is a case in point. Overall, greenhouse gas emissions were reduced by 72% from 1990 levels, also exceeding early targets set at 65% by 2010.

Anticipating emissions regulations and conserving energy were only part of the company's rebirth as a sustainable company. "Environmental performance is part of an all-encompassing internal drive toward true sustainable growth," says Chad Holliday. For evidence for an all-encompassing drive to sustainable growth, consider the following corporate initiatives:

- A new product line since 2000 includes a rising share of bio-based materials such as Sorona® fibers based on a corn-derived monomer

(1,3-propanediol; also known as Bio-PDO™) which enables the polymerized fiber to provide natural stain resistance and ultra-violet (UV) fading protection. DuPont is the lead actor in a Department of Energy (DOE) consortium seeking to make commercial ethanol from cellulosic corn material (the stalks, cobs, and leaves that are left in the field after harvest) and is building a pilot plant to begin production in 2009

- Other "green" products are ultra-low-VOC coatings for the auto industry, eight essential components that go into solar panels, biofuels, green building products such as a special-grade Tyvek® house-wrap to lower CO_2 emissions for European customers, and air and water filtration

- Sales to emerging markets include those in the so-called base-of-the-pyramid markets. Selling to the world's less fortunate is an explicit part of DuPont's emerging-markets strategy through its Solae and Pioneer nutrition and seeds companies. Since much of the world's nutrition and agricultural needs are in the world's poorer regions, it is unsurprising that sales in these markets between 2001 and 2006 increased from 24% to 36% (emerging markets are defined here as markets outside the G7 group of the US, Japan, UK, France, Germany, Italy, and Canada)

DuPont has a long history in agriculture through its sales of agricultural chemicals. Moving into soy-based nutrition and bio-based seeds, facilitated by its Solae and Pioneer ventures, was a natural extension of that business.

Sustainability-driven business results

In addition to the $3 billion in avoided costs through energy conservation and greenhouse gas emission reductions, DuPont's shift to high-value low-energy products is helping to position the company for an increasingly carbon-constrained marketplace. Biofuels, solar panels, fuel cells, and green building products are all soaring as markets anticipate tighter carbon regulations and rising fuel prices.

New revenue streams from sustainability ventures include the sale of greenhouse gas reduction credits, the sale of soy foods and hybrid seeds to meet new health and nutritional needs, and the growth of business in emerging markets including the base of the pyramid.

Corporate image and reputation went from "worst of" to "best of" in less than a decade. DuPont is still grappling with serious issues, chief among them being a chemical called perfluorooctanoic acid (PFOA) used in Teflon, which is scheduled to be phased out by 2015.

DuPont is still targeted by regulators and activists for a range of environmental and health-related impacts of its businesses. However, the image transformation of the company over the last ten years is nothing short of remarkable. In 2005, it was ranked first on *Business Week*'s list of "The Top Green Companies." In 2006, it was awarded "best in class" for its approach to climate change by an investor coalition called the Carbon Disclosure Project. Ironically, it was also the recipient of the Presidential Green Chemistry Award (for its Bio-PDO™ materials) from the US EPA, the very same body that had labeled DuPont the top US polluter in the mid 1990s. For a science company intent on hiring the best and the brightest, its emerging reputation as a sustainable company was of considerable value in human resource terms alone.

DuPont's relationship to environmental legislation went from lobbying to slow down climate change regulation to encouraging such regulation. As a leading sustainable company, DuPont wants to avoid seeing the price of oil drop to $20 a barrel. A mandatory federal cap-and-trade program would be to its advantage. For these reasons, DuPont played a lead role in the early 2007 efforts of the US Climate Action Partnership. Lobbying government regulators for climate change action is a way to shape the marketplace to favor companies offering energy efficiencies, reduced emissions, and renewable-energy products and services.

DuPont's recent financial performance bears out its strategy and suggests that holistic sustainability initiatives are not incompatible with short-term results. Earnings per share (EPS) have risen steadily from –$1.1 in 2002, $1 in 2003, $1.8 in 2004, $2.1 in 2005, $2.8 in 2006, and an estimate of $3.6 in 2007.

Organizational journey

In early 2007 I had the opportunity to discuss DuPont's organizational journey with Dr Paul Tebo, corporate VP for health, safety, and the environment at DuPont between 1993 and 2004. Although his role was one of a sustainability specialist, he was part of the chairman's office. Paul Tebo came from a line management background, earlier having run a $2 billion unit inside DuPont. These factors, combined with his ability to work closely with CEO Chad Holliday, gave him both the credibility and the influence needed to affect change.

I asked Paul what were the key success factors in getting sustainability deeply ingrained in the DuPont organization. Three key success factors in DuPont's case are:

- Unwavering CEO support, initially driven in part by the desire to avoid a negative company reputation and in part by the desire to get ahead of the regulatory curve

- The company-wide integration of sustainability into performance metrics and compensation for key employees including line managers

- Broad external collaboration with stakeholders
  - For example, the partnership with the World Resources Institute (WRI) to meet the company's 10% renewable energy goal
  - For example, the external biotechnology and health advisory boards set up by the company

Linda Fisher, Paul Tebo's successor as corporate vice president and chief sustainability officer, is now bringing a greater customer focus to these issues along the value chain. Working with her is Dawn Rittenhouse, head of sustainable development, who, in 2007, picked up responsibility for DuPont's climate change efforts. With others they are emphasizing new product and market opportunities—a natural evolution in the company's sustainable growth strategy after its earlier phase of cost avoidance and risk mitigation.

DuPont is an example of a mainstream company that is very effective at managing shareholder and stakeholder value in a "win–win" for business and society.

The ability to partner with a broad range of stakeholders is unusual for a science-based company. As the company's CEO said in a speech in November 2006:

> The view of scientists locked away in a laboratory inventing something new and wonderful to spring on the world has given way to a market-back approach. For innovation to be successfully introduced into the marketplace and accepted by society, it must be based on many forms of partnership

and continuous dialog with stakeholders, including governments, NGOs, and academia. Science and innovation that
does not address pressing human needs will not advance sustainability. Likewise a vision of sustainability detached from
science and technology will not succeed. We need both the
commitment to sustainability and the accomplishments of
science.

DuPont's sustainability strategy is an excellent example of an environmentally smart business model for a world marked by growing ecological
disaster. The company's 2015 sustainability goals include doubling
investment in R&D programs that offer direct environmental benefits to
its customers. They include doubling revenues from non-depletable
resources to at least $8 billion. The goals also include growing annual rev-
enues by at least $2 billion from "products that create energy efficiency
and/or significant greenhouse gas emission reductions for our customers." These goals have energized the organization, and engaged
senior executives and line managers in a quest for profitable growth.

6

Wal-Mart

> For Wal-Mart to be successful and continue to grow, we must operate in a world that is healthy and successful . . . we believe that these initiatives and many more to come will make us a more competitive and innovative company, and one that is more relevant to our customers.
>
> *Lee Scott*, CEO, *Wal-Mart Stores, Inc.*

The business world first reacted with disbelief to announcements by Wal-Mart—the world's ultimate low-price, mainstream business player—that it was pursuing sustainability as a core business strategy.[1]

Wal-Mart's four-year-old effort to integrate sustainability into its business model is too recent to declare a success or to point to paradigm-shifting results. However, the company has made it possible to lay out the logic of business sustainability as the next "big idea"—the shift to the next growth-curve 44 years after Sam Walton's original dream of helping people living in small towns in rural America enjoy a similar quality of life to those who live in the big cities.

Wal-Mart's efforts have already succeeded in showing that sustainability can create significant economic value with no net additional costs by driving innovation along supply chains in a variety of unexpected ways. The corporate giant's approach represents an opportunity for the "democratization" of sustainability by shifting to operations and products that are good for the company and for society, creating the fabled win–win and providing Wal-Mart with the prospect, as Lee Scott says, of becoming "a more competitive and innovative company, and one that is more relevant to [its] customers."[2]

It should be noted that the Wal-Mart sustainability initiative described in this chapter addresses primarily environmental issues (related to air, water, soil, climate change, and biodiversity) and not the many social problems for which it has been widely criticized. The company will need to do a better job of integrating the environmental and social aspects of sustainability if it is to gain enduring stakeholder preference in the future.

Wal-Mart's sustainability goals

In October 2005, Wal-Mart publicly declared sustainability as being the gateway to becoming an even better company. It identified three areas for leadership (climate, waste, and sustainable products) and set three audacious goals for the company:

- To be supplied 100% by renewable energy

- To create zero waste

- To sell products that sustain resources and the environment

While aspirational, each goal is bolstered by a specific time-bound objective. For example, Wal-Mart is investing about $500 million a year in technologies and innovation to:

- Reduce greenhouse gases at its existing stores by 20% over the next seven years

- Reduce solid waste from US stores by 25% over the next three years

- Increase the efficiency of its truck fleet by 25% over the next three years

Given that over 90% of Wal-Mart's sustainability footprint[3] is in its supply chain, the biggest potential effect is clearly from the third goal, i.e. selling products that help to conserve resources and sustain the environment. Wal-Mart's ambitious objective aligned with this goal is 20% of its product portfolio in three years.

Wal-Mart is attempting to erase the distinction between being a successful business and a responsible one. For example, its future supply of natural products such as fish can only be sustained if the ecosystems that provide them are sustained. Its promise of "every day low prices" in seafood depends on its access to a robust fishery. Wal-Mart depends on its ability to eliminate waste, use energy efficiently, and avoid the rising costs of substances hazardous to human health and the environment.

As a point of departure, Wal-Mart rejected the premise that sustainability had to increase costs. It began with the assumption that consumers shouldn't have to pay more to get safe, healthful products that sustain the environment. Wal-Mart's sustainability strategies are about the *creation* of economic benefits from improved environmental and social outcomes. So how is Wal-Mart going about delivering sustainable value?

Business opportunities along the value chain

Wal-Mart's sustainability strategies focus squarely on its extended value chain, which includes the value chains of its suppliers as well as its own operations. Wal-Mart is not interested in headquarters-driven corporate social responsibility (CSR) efforts that are disconnected from the business itself. Far from taking a superficial tack, Wal-Mart seeks to embed environmental and social performance in ways that advance its key business priorities.

In many cases, this has involved a four-step process to assess the business risks and opportunities from the often unintended consequences of its activities on the rest of society:

- **Step 1: understand the business priorities** of the merchandise category or product line being assessed. What are the business imperatives that the organization needs to address?

- **Step 2: identify sustainability issues**, the economic, social and environmental trade-offs, and unintended consequences associated with the life-cycle of the product

- **Step 3: identify business activities** along the extended value chain that are linked to the sustainability issues at each stage of the life-cycle, while accounting for their effect on stakeholder[4] value

- **Step 4: identify players** in the value chain undertaking the business activities identified in step 3. In this step, managers assess which players are adding or eroding value for stakeholders at the level of each business activity

Assessing the value created or destroyed through a sustainability lens provides Wal-Mart managers with an opportunity to re-examine the efficiency, effectiveness, and unintended consequences of business activities, as well as the source of value creation and the players affected. Instead of managing only vendors and products, business owners (general merchandizing managers and buyers) are now analyzing the entire value chain from raw materials to a product's end-of-life disposal. In the process, they are uncovering new business opportunities to rethink product choices and procurement processes.

Linking sustainability to business priorities (mapping steps 1 and 2) has been a key to embedding sustainability in the organization. For example, the team charged with addressing sustainability issues for chemical-intensive products had trouble getting traction until it realized that every time products with hazardous ingredients are returned to a Wal-Mart store, the company finds itself hauling hazardous waste with the associated liabilities and extra costs.

The next section looks at organic cotton to illustrate Wal-Mart's new approach.

Organic cotton apparel and soft goods

Cotton is a wonderful natural fiber that, literally, contributes to the fabric of our daily lives. While cotton soft goods are often promoted as natural, healthful products, analyzing the life-cycle of cotton products reveals the potential for many economic, environmental, and social trade-offs with unintended consequences affecting a variety of stakeholders.

The potential to create sustainable value exists by systematically identifying sustainability issues in the product life-cycle, as well as by identifying the individual business activities in the value chain linked to these issues and the supply chain players undertaking these activities.

First, the business priorities of the apparel group were established as a way to ground the sustainability assessment. In step 2 (identifying environmental and social issues within the value chain), the managers of

Wal-Mart's apparel business consulted a variety of economic and social stakeholders along their extended value chain to identify the potential for trade-offs and unintended consequences throughout the product life-cycle. This may be best illustrated by examining the creation and erosion of value associated with the first stage of the product life-cycle—the growing of cotton using traditional agricultural methods.

Like many products produced using "traditional" agricultural methods, growing cotton commonly employs synthetic fertilizers and pesticides including fungicides, herbicides, defoliants, and growth regulators. In California, five of the top nine pesticides (cyanazine, dicofol, naled, propargite, and trifluralin) used in the production of cotton are known carcinogens and may be linked to a multitude of negative health effects, including the increased risk of cancer in communities living near fields managed with these pesticides, as well as the contamination of water and soil, and other negative environmental externalities.[5] Indirect trade-offs may also exist including health risks associated with the use of cotton by-products in the human food chain such as:

- The annual use of more than 500,000 tons of cottonseed oil in salad dressings, baked goods, and snack foods
- The feeding of three million tons of raw cottonseed each year to beef and dairy cattle

In step 3, the managers linked the potential environmental and social issues to specific business activities of their product's extended value chain, and identified the stakeholders associated with the economic, social, and environmental trade-offs. For example, cotton farming creates jobs and generates taxes in agricultural communities, but may also erode the health and quality of life of people within those communities if the use of synthetic pesticides negatively affects the health and wellness of farmers and others living near the fields.

Figure 6.1 presents the value chain activities linked to the key environmental and social issues throughout the product's extended life-cycle.

In step 4, the managers examined the supply chain, linking the activities of value chain corresponding players to each of the key business activities identified in step 3. Once identified, an assessment was made of each player's contribution or erosion to stakeholder value.

By mapping steps 1–4, the managers were able to identify areas of business opportunity to enhance efficiency and optimize value creation from a systems perspective.

Consider a line of V-neck and Capri athletic wear sold through Sam's Club, a wholesale-club retailer and subsidiary of Wal-Mart Stores, Inc.

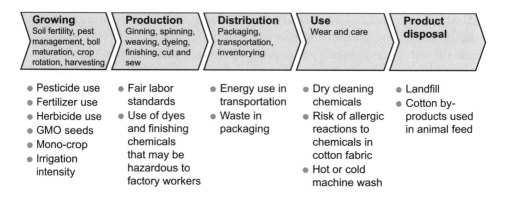

FIGURE 6.1 Sustainability issues in the cotton apparel value chain

When a buyer initially wanted to source organic cotton for these items, she found that clothing vendors were willing to deliver the organic cotton version to specification *but at a substantial increase in cost* compared with the conventional product.

Applying the lens of sustainability to the extended value chain not only identified organic agriculture as a significant opportunity to reduce the unintended consequences associated with cotton products whose raw material was produced using a variety of synthetic inputs, but also forced the managers to examine the strategic value of the company's relationships with economic stakeholders in the value chain, and the effectiveness of its role in the value chain and the efficiency of current business arrangements.

Wal-Mart, like most retailers, has a core competence in sourcing. Yet, in the old way of doing business, it was the manufacturer who was charged with sourcing the cotton raw material. When Wal-Mart built relationships with organic cotton farmers around the world, aggregating demand and sharing know-how with farmers across geographical areas, it was able to create value for the farmers while cutting inefficiencies along the value chain.

By spring 2005, the result was a commercially successful organic cotton version of the V-neck and Capri outfit. These items sold at price parity with the conventional cotton outfit and flew off shelves in all parts of the US—underscoring the strength of the "natural lifestyle" market when consumers are not asked to sacrifice color, style, quality, or price for environmental benefits. Organic cotton apparel sales in the second half of 2005 and first quarter of 2006 allowed Sam's Club to avoid using 1.5 million pounds of synthetic fertilizers, pesticides, herbicides, and defoliants—enough to fill the cargo holds of six 747 jumbo jets.

Because organic cotton farmers represent the bottleneck to expanding sales of organic cotton apparel, Wal-Mart has a strong incentive to build loyal long-term relationships with them. It does so by helping conventional cotton farmers who are interested in switching to organic production to develop a transition strategy to convert conventional fields to organic, including obtaining financing. It helps organic cotton farmers to learn and share best-practice growing techniques. In some cases, Wal-Mart is helping these farmers to commercialize food produce from non-cotton crops grown in crop rotation with cotton.

Once a strong supply base of organic cotton farmers exists, Wal-Mart becomes a supplier to its suppliers, doing what it does best by helping key players to source efficiently at each stage of the cotton apparel's value chain.

The success of value chain optimization is in no small way dependent on sustainability's galvanizing effect on buyers and suppliers. Once engaged in the quest for a more sustainable product, these managers bring new levels of creativity to innovate business solutions. Performance is no longer just about profit, it's about creating financial *and* societal value.

The business case for organic cotton apparel is as persuasive for Wal-Mart as the societal case is for its stakeholders. Product differentiation is the most obvious: at the same color, style, quality, and price, the organic cotton seal becomes a "plus one"—particularly for higher-income consumers who may be attracted to Wal-Mart by such items. Other business benefits include reduced risks from tightening environmental regulations of toxic chemicals, reduced community and NGO opposition, and an enhanced image for Wal-Mart with employees and external stakeholders.

Finally, Wal-Mart's size means it has the opportunity to change the business context of the entire apparel sector. By helping to make organic cotton competitive with conventional cotton, it will revolutionize mainstream consumer expectations with attendant first-mover advantage based on establishing loyal relationships with farmers and the other players who hold the key to organic cotton as a scarce resource.[6]

The TV/DVD combo

Sustainability strategies in the electronics merchandise category led Wal-Mart to redesign a TV/DVD combo to address packaging waste and hazardous substances used in the product manufacture. Units were "right-sized" by improving the cube use, and moving the speakers and some control buttons to the sides in an effort to improve volumetric space.

In addition, Wal-Mart has taken a proactive stance on encouraging electronics suppliers to restrict the use of hazardous substances in the manufacture of their products. These substances include lead, cadmium, mercury, and others identified in the European Union's Restriction of Hazardous Substances (RoHS) Directive 2002/95/EC, which complements the Waste Electrical and Electronic Equipment (WEEE) Directive 2002/96/EC. Although these Directives do not apply in the US, they allow Wal-Mart to harmonize regulatory compliance worldwide and to anticipate stiffer regulations in the US. The results so far:

- Over 400,000 pounds of plastic eliminated through the TV/DVD combo right-sizing

- Six critical hazardous substances designed out

- Drastically improved cube and packaging materials usage by eliminating 45,000 pounds of expanded polystyrene (EPS) packaging foam and 217,000 pounds of corrugated cardboard

These improvements roll up to save the business an estimated $4.3 million annually at the process and risk levels of strategic focus.

The truck auxiliary power unit

Wal-Mart has one of the largest private fleets in the US with over 7,000 Class 8 diesel trucks. In partnership with specialist NGOs and transportation efficiency experts, Wal-Mart reassessed opportunities to increase its fleet fuel efficiency. One such action led to retrofitting each vehicle with an auxiliary power unit (APU). The APU eliminates the use of the tractor's main engine for keeping drivers warm or cool at night, or while stationary during the day. Instead, this very small diesel engine does the job at optimum efficiency and saves a substantial amount of fuel.

The APUs have given Wal-Mart the ability to conform to a corporate nationwide "no-idle" policy—benefiting the communities in which Wal-Mart operates by reducing ground pollution and noise.

The net present value of this investment over the seven-year-life of the APU equipment is estimated to be $68 million. Pro-rated 2006 results[7] are shown below:

- $22.8 million in 2006, and $25.5 million per year thereafter at an average diesel cost of $2.60 per gallon

- Simple payback of less than 2 years

- Eliminates 89,000 tonnes of CO_2 emissions

- Eliminates 75–90% of other harmful airborne emissions

- Eliminates 8 million gallons of diesel fuel

Business value is created at the process level by making in-house fleets more efficient. Additional value comes from anticipating risks associated with greenhouse gas emissions, and from enhancing Wal-Mart's reputation both nationally and at the level of the local communities affected by fleet traffic.

LED-lit refrigerated doors

Wal-Mart is the largest supplier of food in the United States. Refrigerated cases are used extensively in Wal-Mart stores and consume a disproportionate amount of energy in cooling and lighting. Until now, refrigerated cases used fluorescent lighting and had no doors to make them more inviting for customers. Replacing fluorescent lights with LEDs offers a more natural pure white light, while reducing the lighting load by 50%. Because LED lighting is visually superior to fluorescent lighting, Wal-Mart has experimented with adding doors on the cases to reduce the refrigeration load by 30%. Maintenance costs are also dramatically reduced due to the extended life and shock/vibration resistance of LEDs. Finally, the negative disposal impact of mercury in fluorescent lights is eliminated.

A new set of core competencies in the organization

Sustainability strategies are requiring Wal-Mart to adopt new skills to assess and manage the unintended consequences of operations and value chains associated with raw materials, production, distribution, and disposal of merchandise.

In the past, merchants developed skills around managing vendors and products; sustainability strategies now require the development of capabilities to manage value chains using a broader definition of value that includes a societal dimension. The shift in skill-set corresponds to the shift from individual transactions toward conducting business based on leveraged relationships within whole systems.

Retailers now need to go to the players along the supply chain whose business activities best map to the sustainability issues at stake. In partnership with them, retail managers must learn how to optimize the business activities along their extended value chains and choose appropriate players to contract with.

Retailers who develop these new core competencies have an opportunity to reverse the supply chain relationship, selling sustainability management services to suppliers and other players along the product supply chain.

These new competencies are part of a larger corporate leadership challenge. Leaders throughout the organization are being asked to think strategically beyond short-term financial interests to take into account the needs of multiple constituencies. They must be good communicators who operate with humility, candor, and transparency. They are being called on to demonstrate integrity in the face of increasingly difficult decisions that deal with levels of complexity and contradictions that the moguls of the early 20th century—Thomas J. Watson Sr, John D. Rockefeller Jr, Henry Ford, and Charles Kettering to name a few—would be unlikely to even recognize. The "soft skills" of showing empathy, being a good listener, and collaboration have become more critical than ever as business leaders straddle global networks and supply chains.

Lessons learned

Based on the first few years' experience of engaging Wal-Mart's value chain in sustainability strategies, the following lessons have emerged as critical to success:

- Consider sustainability as a source of competitive advantage along the value chain, not as a public relations initiative or bolt-on addition to an existing product or operation. To be a source of competitive advantage, the sustainability "lens" must be applied to the entire value chain associated with the product or operation, and not just to the segment of the value chain associated with the company's activities

- Play offense, not just defense. Use sustainability issues to create new business opportunity, not just to reduce risk

- Learn to collaborate with key stakeholders including those seen as peripheral or adversarial. NGOs and organizations or individuals that are seen as critical of the company frequently have expertise and insights that prove critical to business innovations

- Develop a sustainability pathway based on quick wins, innovations, and game-changing moves. Use quick wins to build organizational momentum to tackle innovations that require greater effort and investment

- Build the organizational capacity and leadership skills required to manage sustainability performance as part of normal business operations. Training in sustainability for executives and line managers can be valuable in transforming the organizational mind-set and building the new skill-set required

Wal-Mart's effort compellingly demonstrates that executives who pay attention to these key success factors will be able to strengthen their business strategies and contribute to more adaptable and robust organizations.

7
Lafarge

Business cannot succeed in a world that fails.

Bertrand Collomb, chairman and former CEO, Lafarge, SA

Company overview

Lafarge, a French-based global industry leader in building materials, has current annual sales of $23 billion and a workforce of 80,000 worldwide. Its main products are cement, roofing, aggregates, concrete, and gypsum. With 2006 operating income of nearly $4 billion, the company has been profitable over most of its history since its founding in 1833.

The main environmental issues for this company are energy efficiency, CO_2 emissions (a significant problem for the entire cement industry), and quarry restoration. Social issues include Lafarge's relationships with local communities as well as employee safety, skills development associated with highly automated plants, and human rights.

About a third of its sales in 2006 were outside western Europe and North America. Of these, over half were in Africa and Asia–Pacific in countries such as Zambia, Morocco, Bangladesh, and China.

Social issues addressed

Lafarge's presence in emerging markets has presented it with a unique set of social challenges. These include:

- Modernizing old cement plants with workforce reductions that often involve many hundreds of employees
- Respecting international labor conventions in countries that have long ignored human rights
- Avoiding corruption practices
- Land use issues with local populations faced with new cement plants or quarries
- In some areas, managing a workforce impacted by a high incidence of HIV/Aids

This chapter addresses three cases of emerging market challenges:

- The relocalization of a village in Bangladesh during the construction of a new cement plant
- The redeployment of employees resulting from the closure of a cement plant in Morocco
- HIV/Aids prevention in Zambia

Principles of action

Lafarge's principles of action—its vision, commitments, and the "Lafarge way"—have guided the company's management in dealing with social issues for the last quarter-century. Lafarge's mission of "being the best" includes a strong stakeholder focus while the emphasis on multi-local management gives geographically dispersed teams the ability to take on autonomous local initiatives.

The company's principles are distributed to every employee and form a type of contract that everyone is expected to respect in their day-to-day work.

Here is an extract from Lafarge's principles of action:

> We will succeed in creating sustainable value by contribut-
> ing to economic, social and environmental progress . . .
> Being the preferred partner for our communities means:

> acting as responsible members of our communities; con-
> tributing to the development of the people, their health,
> rights and well-being by generating economic growth and
> supporting social, educational and cultural advance-
> ment . . .

While the principles of action focus on social responsibility, they also emphasize heavily the need to be the best in terms of customer satisfaction, operational excellence, and shareholder returns. Lafarge's management has a deeply rooted belief that it cannot create societal value without creating enduring financial value.

Social initiatives taken by Lafarge

The following sections provide a short description of the three social initiatives and highlight how they created value for society and value for Lafarge as a business.

Relocalization of a village in Bangladesh

In order to construct a new cement plant at Chhatak in Bangladesh, 72 families (about 350 people) living at the site selected for the project had to be relocated. These included the inhabitants of Tingergaon and adjoining villages around Chhatak, of which 142 were children.

Chhatak presented unique challenges for Lafarge: the cement plant is situated in Bangladesh while the limestone quarry that supplies it is ten miles away in the Indian state of Meghalaya. Aside from the administrative and legal hurdles, Lafarge had to negotiate ownership of the strip of land on which the conveyor belt would run from the quarry in India to the cement plant across the border.

Added to these complexities was the delicate human challenge of relocating the 72 families around the cement plant itself. As is standard practice in such situations, Lafarge began by offering to compensate the villagers with funds for land and housing. However, the company went well beyond financial compensation by developing a program to provide non-formal primary-level education for the children and continuous basic healthcare facilities for all. It also provided vocational training for the adults, particularly women, on different trades to create income-generating opportunities. All these programs were developed in close cooperation with local associations.

Social results for the villagers

There was no school in the village before relocalization. Now the classrooms of the Community Development Center have over 140 children split into four different-level classes. Teachers pursue the government curricula for primary-school education. Books and stationery are provided free of charge to the pupils. In addition, the huge cement plant under construction at Chhatak will contribute to further local economic development. According to chairman Bertrand Collomb, the impact of Lafarge's relocalization initiative is widely perceived as positive by the local inhabitants and contrasts markedly with installations where little or no social investment was made.

Business results for Lafarge

For its investment of $1.5 million in rehabilitation assistance (including setting up the Community Development Center and expenses towards continued education, healthcare, and vocational training), Lafarge benefited from a relatively smooth installation and launch process involving the local workforce. Interestingly, on the Indian side where less effective effort was made to invest in the local community surrounding the quarry, there were occasional incidents of vandalism and workforce disruption. The comparison between the differing social value created on both sides of the border and the respective consequences provide a measure of social impact.

Social actions such as the one at Chhatak contribute to Lafarge's global reputation as a responsible industry leader. They can also contribute to its being the favored candidate to acquire cement plants in competitive or denationalized cases where foreign authorities must assess the desirability of the acquiring companies.

Redeployment of employees at a closed cement plant in Morocco

Faced with an obsolete plant that no longer served the needs of the market, Lafarge decided to close the Tetouan plant and replace it with a modern automated facility. The new plant would employ 99 people (after rehiring and training) instead of the 195 people employed by the old plant.

To carry out its plan, Lafarge decided to implement an employee-centered personnel program consisting of three components:

- Assistance with redeployment at a local company

- Grants to help start the employee's own small business venture (up to $18,000 or 80% of the cost of the venture)

- Transfers and early retirement at age 55

Social results for the downsized employees

After transfers and early retirements, Lafarge helped to find employment solutions for the remaining 121 laid-off workers and ultimately created 266 new jobs through 111 micro-enterprises. "In spite of the inherent difficulties of our project, all our objectives were met . . . and exceeded," says Jean-Marie Schmitz, the general manager of Lafarge Morocco.

"We owe them this consideration and we must comply with the Group's principles of action. This means that nobody must be left out," explains Larbi Koullou, the coordinator of the redeployment plan.

To deal with the challenge, Lafarge Morocco set up a permanent four-man support team, including the plant manager, to facilitate personnel redeployment once the plant closure became official.

The local population touched by the project went from initial skepticism and outright rejection to being strong supporters and having newfound respect for Lafarge for accomplishing what it said it would do.

Business results for Lafarge

In the face of initial resistance to Lafarge's proposed project, the redeployment plan led to a number of business benefits including:

- Stronger partnerships with government authorities (which regulate and issue permits)

- More loyal and better-trained employees (the redeployment plan led to a more rigorous assessment of competencies than would otherwise have existed)

- Better labor union relations

- Improved reputation with local customers

- Preferential status with local suppliers

The new cement plant also avoided many of the pitfalls that renovating the old plant would have incurred. Given the age and obsolete equipment of the old plant and its location near the expanding town of Tetouan, its renovation was neither financially nor environmentally a viable solution.

HIV/Aids prevention in Zambia

In some areas of Zambia, adult HIV/Aids prevalence can be higher than 25% according to the Joint United Nations Program on HIV/Aids (UNAIDS). However, only a third of the population is well informed on the ways to prevent transmission of the virus.

Managers at Lafarge's Chilanga cement plant recognized the negative impact of HIV/Aids on its employees and became committed to protecting their health and safety by establishing appropriate interventions. Lafarge now partners with ZHABS (a Zambia HIV/Aids business sector project) to provide a program on HIV prevention and care in both the workplace and the community. It approved an HIV/Aids policy with the help of ZHABS, the comments of employees and partner organizations, and Integrated Healthcare Consulting (IHC).

Chilanga's prevention program relies on 44 workplace and 24 community peer educators as its primary method. This corresponds to one peer educator for every ten employees, and one community educator for every 100 community members in Musamba. Chilanga also encourages peers to implement similar workplace prevention programs. Employees and their families have access to screening for tuberculosis and treatment of opportunistic infections.

Social results for the employees and local communities

The project has improved knowledge about the risks of HIV/Aids and led to a decline in high-risk behavior that has reduced the incidence of the disease. The Chilanga cement plant and ZHABS are now extending the program to other communities where the company operates.

Business results for Lafarge

The investment amounted to $48,000 including:

- Financial investment by Chilanga of $15,600 and by ZHABS of $22,000

- Donation in kind: Chilanga provides condoms, rent-free office space, and training facilities, while ZHABS provides allowances and uniforms for the peer educators, a salary for the community coordinator, training, and frequent monitoring and supervisory visits

The return on investment for Lafarge is in the form of lower costs associated with the disease. These costs include:

- Leave and absenteeism
- Productivity loss
- Loss of workforce morale
- Management burden
- Production disruptions
- Retirement and disability
- Medical care for the treatment of opportunistic diseases
- High turnover
- Recruitment and training of replacement staff lost through illness

While it is difficult (and perhaps undesirable) to quantify the true cost savings of HIV/Aids prevention, it is obvious from the relatively small investment and the relatively huge impacts of the program that the benefits to Lafarge and to the local communities offer an indisputable "win–win."

Organizational journey

Initially all three initiatives met with skepticism from local employees and stakeholders.

In the case of the Tetouan redeployment plan in Morocco, the support team got down to work in a social atmosphere fraught with doubt. "We had to deal with complaints, feelings of unfairness, and fear of the unknown," recounts project manager Mohamed Tassafout. "In this area, which is subject to heavy unemployment, finding a new job, to say nothing of finding one that offers the same benefits as a job with Lafarge

Morocco, is very difficult." To deal with demand for redeployment services, the support team took things step by step, meeting each person for a number of interviews. "We performed a market research survey to identify business niches," explains Omar Achaach. "We then factored in our knowledge of the area, the workers, their family situations, and the amount of their redundancy packages." Such a comprehensive redeployment approach was a first in Morocco. "Normally, companies just hand employees their severance pay without redeployment. The strength of Lafarge is it has encouraged its employees to set up family-run businesses, and so create more jobs," concludes Larbi Koullou.

In the case of the Chhatak cement plant in Bangladesh, a very personal role was played by Shabbir Hossain, director of the Resettlement Action Plan (RAP). He was responsible for the various programs for training, resettlement, primary-school education, and establishment of health clinics, and became personally involved with many of the families. "It was part of my responsibility. For example, I helped several individuals open new bank accounts. I negotiated land purchases for them . . . in general, I committed to being always there for them."

For Lafarge, the following key success factors were apparent across these three initiatives:

- **Transparency and early communication.** In the case of the closure of the Tetouan cement plant, the decision was made to inform the personnel and labor unions a full two years in advance. In all three cases, dedicated teams were put into place early on to identify all potential issues and to carry out the planned projects

- **Partnership with local stakeholders.** In the case of the Chilanga cement plant's HIV/Aids prevention initiative, local partners such as ZHABS played a key role in gaining local acceptance and credibility for the actions undertaken. The local provincial authority (or Wilaya) and the village elders played a key role in the case of the Tetouan redeployment plan. Local associations cooperated with Lafarge at every step of the Bangladesh Chhatak project

- **Adaptation to local culture.** The approach to dealing with disruptive change requires leadership that is accepted in the context of the local culture. According to Lafarge, "the region of Tetouan is impregnated with a sense of honor [that] accords a primary place to personal courage and respect for a person's word. By coming in person to announce to the employees the closure of the plant, by writing to each employee personally, and committing to help them, the General Manager [of Lafarge Morocco] acted as an honorable man, therefore worthy of respect and confidence"

- **CEO/senior executive commitment.** Social responsibility succeeds on the ground in Lafarge because of the cascading engagement of its senior leaders from its chairman to country general managers, local plant managers, and HR directors, bound together by the company's principles of action

Lafarge, a profitable global industry leader, provides an excellent "social value" example of corporate leadership for world benefit. With its global culture of social responsibility, it succeeds in creating value for local stakeholders in ways that ultimately allow it to be a more successful and more competitive company.

8

NatureWorks LLC, a subsidiary of Cargill

The packaging industry is coming to realize that deciding to use an annually renewable material is only the first step. To reach maximum benefit, the supply chain partners and brand owner must strategically address the design and manufacturing of the pack . . . Planning for the environmentally sound post-consumer disposal or recovery of the package is essential.

Dennis McGrew, president and CEO of NatureWorks LLC

NatureWorks overview

Based in Minnesota with manufacturing facilities in Blair, Nebraska, NatureWorks LLC is a stand-alone company wholly owned by Cargill. Cargill is an international provider of food, agricultural, and risk management products and services with 124,000 employees in 59 countries.

Started in 1997 as a 50:50 joint venture between Cargill and The Dow Chemical Company, Cargill Dow LLC became NatureWorks LLC on January 24, 2005, when Cargill bought out Dow's interest in the venture. Nature-Works LLC employs approximately 230 people: 100 expert plant technicians, 35 research and development specialists, and almost 100 commercial people.

NatureWorks LLC is the first company to offer nearly greenhouse-gas-neutral polymers on a commercial scale derived from 100% annually renewable resources with a cost and performance that compete with petroleum-based packaging materials and fibers. It offers its customers a meaningful way to help achieve compliance with the Kyoto Protocol for the reduction of greenhouse gases.

The company applies its unique technology to the processing of natural plant sugars to create a proprietary polylactide polymer, which is marketed under the NatureWorks® polymer and Ingeo® fiber brand names.

NatureWorks® polymer is made from lactic acid (see Figure 8.1), a naturally occurring substance produced in this case from a wholly renewable resource—currently corn. Growing corn takes CO_2 and water from the earth and the air, and makes carbon through photosynthesis. The carbon in the corn is in the form of starch. The NatureWorks process converts the starch to sugar, and the sugar is fermented into lactic acid. The polymer is used in:

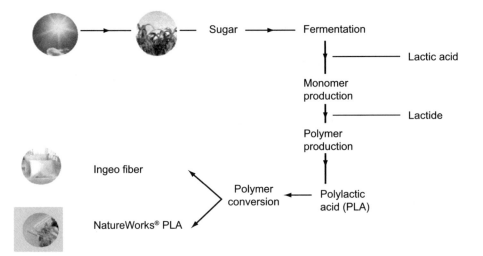

FIGURE 8.1 The NatureWorks polylactic acid (PLA) production process

- Packaging and other plastics applications marketed under the NatureWorks® brand

- Fiber applications which are marketed under the Ingeo™ brand

The characteristics obtained with the plastic resin are similar to those of petroleum-based plastics and can be used in a wide range of applications including bottles, disposable service ware, durable goods, containers, trays, and films as well as apparel, home textiles, and non-woven applications such as baby wipes and diapers.

The current situation: petroleum-based packaging

Conventional plastics are derived from petroleum or natural gas, with the bulk coming from petroleum. Production of conventional plastics uses more than 180 million barrels of oil per year. Roughly 7–10% of the fossil fuel consumed in the US is used to manufacture plastics and fibers. Among the petroleum-based plastics is polyethylene terephthalate (PET), a popular plastic used in packaging and one that can be recycled. According to the National Association for PET Container Resources (NAPCOR), the PET recycling rate in the US increased to 21.6% in 2004 and the collected volume of PET post-consumer containers exceeded 1 billion pounds—a record. In addition, "the use of post-consumer recycled PET increased 59% from 2003 to 2004 to a record 878 million pounds."[1]

But, while these higher recycling rates are promising, the majority of PET containers are not being recycled. Millions of pounds of PET packaging end up in US landfills each year where they will stay virtually forever as the decomposition rate of PET is millions of years.

The opportunity for petroleum substitutes

Due to the increased cost of petroleum, food packagers in 2005 faced price hikes of 30–80% for conventional plastics. In more practical terms, these increases have equated to prices being raised 8–10 times in 2005. As a result, companies are passing on their costs, e.g. Kraft Foods announced in November 2005 that it would increase the price of many products by an average of nearly 4%.

Beyond rising oil prices, the industry is also faced with issues of scarcity and rising waste disposal costs. US petroleum imports continue to rise, yet experts agree that our oil supplies will run short within the next 20–60 years. The cost of waste disposal—both by landfilling and incineration—is rising everywhere.

The business risks for food packers and retailers have created an opportunity for NatureWorks LLC. Large-volume retailers such as Wal-Mart Stores Inc. are shifting their attention to sustainable packaging alternatives. One example is Wal-Mart's recent sourcing of thermoformed packaging for its food products. This first stage of new packaging translated into 100 million plastic containers a year or the equivalent of saving 800,000 gallons of gasoline.

Environmental and business benefits of the NatureWorks packaging

The NatureWorks plant opened in Blair, Nebraska, in 2002 with a theoretical annual capacity to produce 300 million pounds of resin. The polymer can be made into performs that can be molded on standard PET performs systems. Use of the renewable plant-based feedstock instead of petroleum means that NatureWorks LLC consumes up to 68% less fossil fuel to produce the biopolymer and generates up to 68% fewer greenhouse gas emissions than conventional plastics. Table 8.1 summarizes the environmental benefits of using NatureWorks® polymer.

Nevertheless, NatureWorks LLC still uses fossil fuels to run the plant where it processes the polymer. To address this issue, the company purchased enough Renewable Energy Certificates (RECs) in 2005 to offset all the non-renewable energy used for the entire 2006 production of NatureWorks® polymer—thus making NatureWorks the world's first greenhouse-gas-neutral polymer.

In addition, NatureWorks polymer-based packaging has the flexibility to be disposed of in several ways, including recycling and composting, and fits most local waste disposal schemes. NatureWorks polymer is certified by the Biodegradable Products Institute (BPI) as compostable, and items and components made of NatureWorks polymer can be successfully

	NatureWorks®	Olefins	PET	PTT	Nylons
Fossil energy consumption vs. NatureWorks® polymer					
Total energy consumption index	1.0	1.3–1.4	1.4	1.3–1.5	2.1–2.4
Percentage from renewable sources	56	1 to ≥ 2	≤1	0–17	≤1
Greenhouse gas (CO_2 equivalent generation vs. NatureWorks® polymer)					
GHG generation index	1.0	1.2–1.3	2.0	1.6–2.3	4.5–5.5

PET = polyethylene terephthalate; PTT = polytrimethylene terephthalate

TABLE 8.1 Estimated environmental benefits of replacing petroleum-based polymers with NatureWorks® polymer

composted in applications where that disposal method is desired and a commercial composting infrastructure is in place.

When the NatureWorks polymer decomposes, it turns into carbon dioxide and water rather than sitting forever in a landfill. Under the controlled heat and humidity conditions of an industrial composting facility, the polymer will dissolve within months. The polymer's multiple disposal features mean it can also play a key role in landfill diversion. According to former CEO of NatureWorks LLC, Kathleen Bader, "We're using material that's renewable in 100 days instead of 100 million years."

In addition, NatureWorks LLC took a step that most other polymer manufacturers do not do: it brought in a third-party company to perform a life-cycle assessment (LCA) of the total energy used to create the polymer, from buying and planting the seed, to the gas used to run farm equipment such as tractors, to the pellet leaving the manufacturing gate. The results of the study show that NatureWorks polymer uses significantly less energy during its life-cycle than traditional petroleum-based packaging.

Finally, NatureWorks LLC is committed to working with its customers to provide them with the type of packaging that best fits their needs and values. For example, some companies and regions do not want to purchase goods that contain genetically modified organisms (GMOs). Because NatureWorks polymer comes from local farmers, its general feedstock is a mix of both GMO and non-GMO corn, depending on what kind of seed the local farmers plant each year. However, the polymer itself does not contain any GMOs as the corn is completely destroyed during processing.

Nevertheless, according to Snehal Desai, "GMO corn is really about the seed, and it is a big, complicated, agricultural issue. Even though our PLA pellets do not contain GMOs, we have crafted three source options that our customers can pay a premium to select." These options are as follows:

- Third-party certification verifying the absence of genetic material in the resin

- A source offset program linking customers and farmers

- Identity-preserved polymer where customers can verify the source of the dextrose and the absence of genetic material through all steps of resin production

When Cargill launched its factory in 2002, its pellets were far more expensive than equivalent material made from petroleum. Wild Oats Markets, an early customer, paid 50% more for takeout containers made from the bio-plastic, but attributed a 12% increase in sales within the first months to its new "natural" packaging. Over the next two years, the Cargill plant became more efficient in driving costs out of its own process, accompanied by soaring oil prices for competitors. The result was that, in 2004, the "corn-tainers" in the deli at Wild Oats cost 5% less than traditional plastic according to Wild Oats spokeswoman Sonja Tuitele.

Figure 8.2 shows the price of PLA resin compared with prices for petroleum-based resins from quarter 4 in 2004 to quarter 4 in 2005.

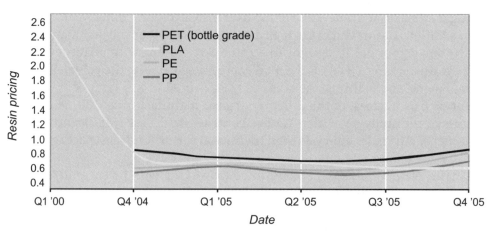

PLA resin pricing is based on larger-volume programs and is grade-specific. PP (polypropylene), PE (polyethylene), and PET resin pricing courtesy of Chemical Market Associates, Inc. (CMAI)

FIGURE 8.2 **PLA resin price in the US compared with petroleum-based resin prices**

In 2005 and early 2006, the company saw rapid marketplace adoption by innovative companies globally, reduced the cost-per-pound to be more competitive with petroleum-based polymers, and experienced significant sales increases and quarter-to-quarter growth. The number of customers more than doubled during the same period with more than 45,000 retail stores worldwide selling products packaged in NatureWorks polymer or goods made of Ingeo™ fiber. In 2005, NatureWorks LLC experienced sales growth of 230%.

Finally, NatureWorks LLC maintains a first-to-market advantage in an industry where some are predicting that "the market for biodegradable packaging will grow by about 20% a year." Instead of seeing new entrants into the market as competitors, NatureWorks LLC sees itself at this early stage in a collaborative role, considering that now is a perfect opportunity to further expand the size of the natural biopolymer market itself.

Organizational journey

NatureWorks polymer began in the late 1980s in a laboratory at Cargill when Pat Gruber, a bench chemist, asked, "What else can we do with corn?" At the time, corn was one of Cargill's commodity products but was used only as the niche polymer made into the dissolvable stitches for sutures. This commodity was incredibly expensive because it was only made in very small quantities. Pat Gruber was the first to ask, "Can we make this a very large commodity product? What would we have then?"

After conducting the due diligence for scaling up and constantly asking "what if . . . ?" Cargill decided it could contribute the fermentation expertise required for the processing, but that it needed someone else to create the polymers and to create the market for it. At this point, The Dow Chemical Company joined Cargill in a joint venture lasting until 2004, when Dow divested NatureWorks (along with several other ventures) as part of a strategic move to redirect its business towards two joint-venture plans in the Middle East.

Research and development from the National Institute of Standards and Technology (NIST) Advanced Technology Program (ATP) and the DOE biomass supported the development of PLA—a limited but important accelerator of the innovation process. When the plant was up and running, and NatureWorks LLC grew in scale, the company determined that it needed a culture change. According to Ann Tucker, the previous director of public affairs, "For most of our life as a company, we were a technically driven organization. We have very brilliant people here, but it was purely science. We had tons of patents but weren't necessarily in touch with what the customer wanted. In many ways, we had a language issue."

So in 2004, the organization brought in Kathleen Bader, a charismatic and highly directive leader (who at the time was the highest-ranking female ever at Dow) to shift the culture from a research-science culture to a customer-oriented, commercially driven organization. In many ways, Kathleen Bader was the turnaround specialist charged with shaking up the organization and overhauling the culture of NatureWorks LLC (Cargill Dow at the time).

Her main changes involved modifying scientists' research agendas by cutting the list of projects being worked on to only those that were important to customers and for developing the market. She altered the overall development agenda to ensure that the technology programs under way were the ones customers wanted, not just programs "we thought we could do."

Part III
The sustainable value toolkit

[Sustainability has] been amazingly good for [Interface's] business. Its costs are down, not up . . . Its products are the best they have ever been because sustainable design has provided an unexpected wellspring of innovation. Its people are galvanized around a shared higher purpose . . . And the goodwill in the marketplace generated by this initiative exceeds, by far, what any amount of advertising or marketing expenditure could have generated. This company believes it has found a better way to earn bigger profits—a better business model.

Ray Anderson, founder and chairman, Interface Inc.

How can executives and line managers in the world's leading companies create sustainable value? What is a practical approach to sustainability that they can use to advance business priorities in their own organizations?

Part III outlines a process that managers can use to pursue sustainability-driven innovation for competitive advantage. The process and tools are designed to capture the stakeholder dimension in a way that contributes to business value. The sustainable value approach creates whole-system change that aligns multiple stakeholders on the company's business strategy, providing more robust results than sustainability efforts led by specialized departments working in silos with limited involvement of outside stakeholders.

The process and tools presented in Part III have been used successfully with thousands of executives in the US, Europe, and Asia. The material reflects their insights into what works in creating sustainable value, and what does not. The author is deeply grateful for the contributions these executives have made to the following body of work.

9

Introduction to sustainable value

Creating sustainable value is a way for companies to advance their business priorities, drive innovation, and achieve competitive advantage. Doing so in today's competitive context requires leading companies to carefully consider the social and environmental dimensions of their business activities.

At the core of the idea lies an expanded definition of value that includes value for stakeholders previously marginalized by corporations. This chapter introduces the concept of stakeholder value and reframes it in terms of business value. The sustainable value framework is outlined and illustrated. In the new perspective, "societal" stakeholders such as environmental NGOs and local communities are viewed as potential business partners rather than as illegitimate adversaries; stakeholder value becomes a source of competitive advantage rather than only a moral obligation.

As described in Chapter 4, the need for a sustainable value approach reflects the emergence of a new, stakeholder-rich competitive environment. The growth of stakeholder power has been driven by quantum increases in information combined with rising societal expectations about health and the environment, leading to a tighter interface between business and civil society.[1] Consumers, employees, investor groups, and NGOs—to name just a few stakeholders—are now able to instantly, and globally, access data about any company. Their power to act on the information lies in the growing role of their relationships and other intangibles, such as goodwill, that drive business value.

The rising importance of intangibles in determining stock price is now well documented by economists.[2] Today over 70% of a company's market capitalization is driven by intangibles such as reputation, goodwill, and stakeholder relationships. By comparison, one hundred years ago 70% was based on tangibles such as plant, property, equipment, and hard financial assets.

For all these reasons, the need to take a systematic approach to managing stakeholder impacts has become an important business challenge in addition to a moral one.

The concept of stakeholder value

The core concept behind the framework is that the business value created by a company is always associated with a stakeholder value that can be either positive or negative. Value is created when a business adds to the capital or well-being of its stakeholders. It is destroyed when a business reduces their capital or undermines their well-being.

Executives often ask who defines value for stakeholders. They are confronted with a bewildering array of sources that claim to know what is good for society and the environment. In some cases, government regulators define it. Black box warnings on prescription medication are a way for regulators to signal product issues affecting human health. "Eco-labels" such as the United States Department of Agriculture (USDA)'s Organic Seal, the European Union's Flower, Germany's Blue Angel, and Japan's Eco-Mark provide industry standards of environmental and social value. Socially Responsible Investment (SRI) ratings agencies such as Innovest provide benchmark assessments for investors. Scientific reports and research studies—often sponsored by the companies themselves—provide yet another source of information, as do consumer groups and NGOs.

Ultimately, the most important measure of stakeholder value is the *perception* of value. The individual and collective perception of a given stakeholder group is as important as the technical and scientific "reality" that the company projects about its products. Companies such as Monsanto and Aventis, in the case of genetically modified organisms, learned the hard way that pushing science in the face of stakeholder fears is not productive. Mobile phones with electromagnetic frequency radiation and polyvinyl chloride (PVC) plastics with dioxin issues are both cases in which entire industries have attempted—unsuccessfully—to use science to quell emotion-based perceptions of environmental, social, or health risks.

Example from the construction materials sector

Consider the following example of an aggregates company (mining sand and stone for the construction sector) and the business value of its relationship to local communities and NGOs. It faces two very different scenarios.

- **Scenario 1: the negative stakeholder value case.** The aggregates company operates quarries in ways that negatively affect the local community and ecologies through dust, vibration, visual and noise pollution, and poorly restored spent quarry lands. It does only what is required to comply with government regulations and local permitting authorities. There is little or no communication or coordination with the local community and NGOs

- **Scenario 2: the positive stakeholder value case.** The company operates its quarries with standards for dust, vibration, visual screens, and noise control that are *beyond* compliance levels. It uses landscaping such as planting trees and bermed banks of earth to mitigate the impacts of quarry operations. It restores spent quarry lands through a reforestation and rehabilitation plan that is co-designed with the local community. It works in partnership with NGOs to resolve ecological pressures coming from its operations

In the positive stakeholder value case, the aggregates company can benefit from more favorable permitting terms (faster permit approvals for extensions) and permits of longer duration. Having good relations with local authorities may allow the company to site its quarries closer to urban markets. Positive stakeholder value can also reduce the risk of NGO and community opposition to quarrying activities. Beyond-compliance restoration leads to higher land values once the spent quarry site is sold.

All these benefits translate directly into higher earnings power.

Expanding the value horizon

Historically, business has ignored stakeholder value as a source of competitive advantage, preferring to rely on ownership rights and access to resources as key determinants of its wealth-generating capacity. The problem of value creation now requires reframing in a way that goes beyond issues of access to capital, labor, technology, and location.

In 1980, Michael Porter's *Competitive Strategy: Techniques for Analyzing Industries and Competitors*[3] helped transform the meaning of business value away from ownership rights and resource access, and toward one driven by industry dynamics and industry structure. Value creation came to be seen in terms of:

- The threat of new entrants and substitute products
- Negotiating power with buyers and suppliers
- Industry rivalry

Now the need is to expand further the concept of value creation to include a broader array of stakeholders who contribute to a company's wealth-creating capabilities. The concept of sustainable value expands the value-creating universe to all key stakeholders including societal stakeholders such as NGOs and social activists (many with blogs that reach a wide audience) who have traditionally been ignored or relegated to the fringes by management.

The sustainable value framework

Stakeholder value requires managers to think "outside–in" about how their companies create and sustain competitive advantage. Outside–in thinking, which sees the world from the perspective of stakeholders, is a powerful new lens through which managers can discover new business opportunities and risks. Leaders who engage stakeholders and proactively address stakeholder issues can better anticipate changes in the business environment. They can reduce the risk of being unpleasantly surprised by emerging societal expectations.[4] Ultimately, stronger stakeholder engagement allows leading companies to discover new sources of value through innovation.

Business leaders are familiar with managing financial value, whether in terms of economic value added (EVA)[5] or other measures driving stock price performance. They are less knowledgeable about measuring and managing stakeholder value. Because a company's impacts on stakeholders are often unintentional, it faces hidden risks and opportunities that managers can no longer afford to ignore. To succeed in a stakeholder-driven business environment, business leaders must think and operate in new ways, shaping strategies and actions with full awareness of their impacts on key stakeholders along their value chains.

Figure 9.1 describes company performance along two axes—shareholder value *and* stakeholder value. Managing in two dimensions represents a fundamental shift in how managers think about business performance. In this framework, companies that deliver value to shareholders while destroying value for other stakeholders have a fundamentally flawed business model. Those that create value for stakeholders are cultivating sources of extra value that can fuel competitive advantage for years to come. Sustainable value occurs only when a company creates value that is positive for its shareholders and its stakeholders.

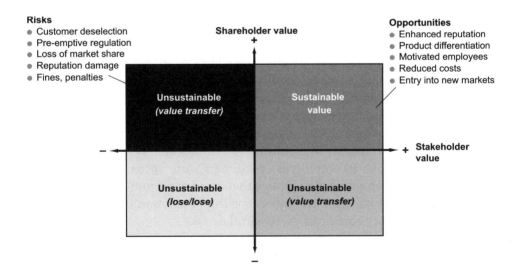

FIGURE 9.1 **The sustainable value framework**

Source: From *The Sustainable Company* by Chris Laszlo. Copyright © 2005 by the author. Reproduced by permission of Island Press, Washington, D.C.

Insight into sustainable value

Rising societal expectations means that a business unit or product that was seen as creating stakeholder value in the past may in the future come to be seen as destroying it, even though the company made little or no change to its product design or business activities. In terms of Figure 9.1, the horizontal axis 'drifts left' over time.

It is possible for a business unit or product to destroy stakeholder value (left-hand side of Figure 9.1) and still be fully compliant with all laws and regulations.

Sustainable value is not about creating stakeholder value at the expense of shareholder value (bottom right-hand quadrant of Figure 9.1). NGOs and social activists who want companies to contribute to society and the environment in ways that require the company to destroy shareholder value fail to understand the nature of business.

Starting in the upper left of Figure 9.1 and moving counterclockwise, consider the following four cases of value creation and destruction.

Upper left quadrant

When value is transferred from stakeholders to shareholders, the stakeholders represent a risk to the future of the business. Leaded paint and asbestos are historical examples; today phthalates in cosmetics and toxic additives in children's toys, volatile organic compounds in carpet adhesives and paints, heavy metals in fabric dyes, and lead solder and brominated flame retardants in consumer electronics are examples of products that create risks to employees, customers, and society while creating value for shareholders. Companies that avoid environmental regulations in their home markets through exporting production to countries with lower regulatory standards create similar risks.

Also in this quadrant are companies that create shareholder value through a low-cost strategy that tolerates management actions to cut costs through avoiding overtime pay, under-training on employee safety, or discriminating on the basis of gender and ethnic background. Shareholder value in these cases is created "on the backs" of one or more stakeholder groups, thereby representing a value transfer rather than true value creation.

Companies with high levels of greenhouse gas emissions face new and rising financial risks. Being perceived as contributing to climate change is increasingly seen as a case of value transfer from stakeholders to shareholders. Companies can no longer operate as if putting carbon into the atmosphere were free. After TXU (Texas's largest electric utility) announced its plan to build 11 new coal-fired power plants in April 2006, its largest shareholders (including CalPERS and the New York City Comptroller's Office) began organizing opposition based on the financial risks related to climate change. Risks included impending federal climate change regulation that would impose new costs on carbon dioxide emissions, and energy efficiency measures that would reduce consumer demand for new power. The activism led the February 2007 buy-out of TXU by two private equity companies to cancel eight of the 11 coal-fired power plants that TXU had planned,[6] signaling for many the beginning of a new era for investment calculations in the energy sector.[7]

Bottom left quadrant

When value is destroyed for both shareholders and stakeholders, this represents a "lose/lose" situation of little interest to either. Monsanto and its European competitor Aventis lost large sums of money by underestimating consumer and farmer resistance to their GMO crop products. Before Aventis sold its CropSciences division to Bayer, it is estimated to have lost $1 billion in buy-back programs and other costs associated with its genetically modified corn StarLink. StarLink was approved only for use in animal feed, but was found by NGOs to have contaminated a number of human food products.

Bottom right quadrant

When value is transferred from shareholders to stakeholders, the company incurs a fiduciary liability to its shareholders. Actions intended to create stakeholder value that destroy shareholder value put into question the company's viability. Environmentalists often unintentionally pressure companies to take actions in this quadrant without realizing that the pursuit of loss-making activities is not sustainable either. Avoiding offshore sourcing to protect American jobs is an example of creating stakeholder value (employee job security) while destroying shareholder value (higher operating costs). Campaigns to "keep jobs in America" may create short-term benefits for American workers but, in most cases, they hurt the companies which end up with uncompetitive labor costs.

It is interesting to note that philanthropy, when it is unrelated to business interests and represents pure charity, is also located in this quadrant. In such a case, philanthropy is implicitly a decision to take financial value from the company's shareholders and to transfer it to one or more of its stakeholders.[8]

Upper right quadrant

When value is created for stakeholders as well as shareholders, stakeholders can represent a potential source of hidden business value. Sustainable value is created only in this case. When companies design manufacturing facilities to use less energy and that cost less to build and operate than conventional facilities, they are creating sustainable value. The same is true when they eliminate packaging waste by right-sizing their products, or when they add environmental intelligence to their products by making them more recyclable, re-usable, biodegradable, less toxic, or otherwise healthier.

Sustainable value is also created when companies find ways to profitably meet unmet societal needs such as by providing nutrition and clean water to the poor. The key is to provide environmental and social benefits to stakeholders without asking customers to trade off higher prices (or poorer quality.) Companies that are global industry leaders cannot afford to require their customers to pay the "green premium" that specialty companies like Patagonia historically charged for their products. Only through innovation and process or product redesign can leading companies create new business and societal benefits without consumer trade-offs.

Creating sustainable value in the automobile industry

This section provides an illustration of expanding the value horizon in the automotive industry. Because of the fossil fuel consumption and greenhouse gas emissions of today's nearly one billion vehicles on the world's roads, their use is one of the most environmentally damaging activities in the world. It is only natural that industry leaders offering a way to reduce, in an economical way, the automobile's negative impacts on society and the environment should find financial rewards. Although the transition to "clean and green" personal transportation is still in its early stages, the business case for it is becoming central to competitive survival in the industry. Toyota and Honda's outperformance relative to General Motors, Ford, and DaimlerChrysler is at least in part attributable to better products that meet rising expectations for fuel efficiency and environmental responsibility.

Today senior managers in charge of running Toyota's business might reasonably conclude that they are doing a good job in creating stake-holder value: their products move their customers and their families, haul materials, and provide other personal mobility solutions. Toyota's vehicles are safe, fuel-efficient, and highly recyclable. Although not everyone would agree, a large number of people in the world might support the view—publicly promoted by the company itself—that Toyota benefits society. Indeed, the record is impressive, whether measured in terms of improvements in fuel efficiency and safety, in customer satisfaction, in comfort and road performance, or in percentage of junked automotive parts that can be recycled. Furthermore, Toyota has consistently created high shareholder value, posting $14 billion in profits for the fiscal year 2007, the highest profit level in the industry.

But, when those same managers look 20 years into the future, a different picture emerges. Stakeholder impacts loom darkly on the horizon, and the current batch of incremental improvements in automotive technology does nothing to dispel the managers' worry. Consider what we know about how internal combustion engine (ICE) cars and trucks impact society and the environment—and then project 20 years forward to a time when an expected 600 million additional vehicles are expected to be on the world's roads, reaching as many as 1.5 billion vehicles in total.

Negative stakeholder impacts begin with the relatively low energy efficiency (about 35%) of the ICE itself. Additional negative impacts are the result of a chassis design that combines the ICE with predominantly mechanical systems for steering, braking, and throttling. Cars typically weighing 3,000 pounds or more are designed to move four (or fewer) people, contributing to energy inefficiency as well as to safety risks, noise, and urban congestion.

Supply chain risks for car companies are increasingly linked to the environmental and social impacts of their suppliers, which can translate into higher component costs or even reputation damage. For example, suppliers of steel, aluminum, rubber, and plastics are all likely to be affected by greenhouse gas emission regulations. Component suppliers with greater carbon intensity will be at a relative disadvantage to those that offer comparable components with lower carbon intensity.[9]

For the industry as a whole, the manufacture and use of its products translates into the following environmental and social impacts:

- Emissions of greenhouse gases, particularly carbon dioxide, contributing to global warming

- The formation of ground-level ozone and smog resulting in health issues such as asthma

- Other chemical releases such as nitrogen oxides adding to air pollution

- Solid waste and water contamination generated in the manufacture of steel, batteries, paints, plastics, and lubricants

- Safety risks from heavy and mechanically complex vehicle designs

- Unsustainable resource use. The automotive sector is a significant contributor to the depletion of fossil fuels, consuming between a third and a half of the world's oil when the manufacturing process is included

In contrast, "clean energy" drivetrains such as hydrogen fuel cells are twice as energy-efficient as their ICE counterparts and emit nothing more than water vapor. Although it takes energy to extract hydrogen from sources such as oil, natural gas, and ethanol, the fuel cell's high efficiency more than compensates for the energy required to accomplish the extraction. And, eventually, the energy required to produce the hydrogen for fuel cells will come from renewable sources such as cellulosic biomass, hydroelectricity, solar, wind, or geothermal energy.

When integrated with drive-by-wire technology, cars and trucks can be designed to be much lighter. The design has fewer constraints because a mechanical drivetrain is no longer needed. The freeing-up of space and weight contribute to a potentially safer, more comfortable, more personalized, less expensive vehicle. In the General Motors (GM) conception, drive-by-wire fuel cell vehicles (called Hy-wire, for hydrogen-by-wire) consist of an integrated skateboard-like chassis containing the fuel cell, electric drive motor, hydrogen storage tanks, electronic controls, heat exchangers, and braking and steering systems. The vehicle's body sits on top of the chassis, fitted together much like plug-and-play computer components. A simple visit to the dealer could enable the owner to pop up the existing body—say, a sports sedan—and replace it with another body such as a minivan, while keeping the same chassis. From the consumer's perspective, it's somewhat analogous to being able to switch the bezels on a Swatch watch—you get several interchangeable models with one base unit.

Although the financial returns of mass-producing drive-by-wire fuel cell vehicles remain unproven, it is possible to discern the logic of increasing shareholder value from improved stakeholder value. Consumers who value the clean emissions, fuel efficiency, safety, comfort, and personalized designs of such vehicles will eventually pay more for them as the costs of air pollution and climate change rise. The higher starting torque also provides a classic performance benefit—faster acceleration from stationary.

Clean-energy vehicle manufacturers will also benefit from raw materials savings and the lower capital intensity inherent in the greater design freedom afforded by the drive-by-wire and stackable fuel cell technologies. Modular design could lower development costs through economies of scale of the base chassis models required to fit multiple body types. Having a smaller variety of components (such as can be achieved with fuel cell stacks that can be scaled up or down) will further reduce costs.

Shareholder value will be created for those companies that succeed in shaping the automobile industry's rules of the game in their favor and who are better prepared for sudden shifts in regulatory requirements. Legislation such as California's AB32, mandating a 25% reduction in carbon dioxide emissions by 2020, foreshadows a national mandatory cap-and-trade scheme in the US. In a carbon-constrained world, car manufacturers that achieve a cost advantage in low (or zero) emission technologies will find that they have a significant new competitive advantage.

While the fuel cell vehicle remains commercially unproven, Toyota's growing portfolio of hybrid models is an example of successful product design that effectively integrates stakeholder considerations. Yet the success of the Prius and other hybrid models is hardly a decision by the company to suddenly "go green." By some measures, Toyota's overall environmental performance improvements are unimpressive. Between 1990 and 2005, Toyota's new fleet average CO_2 emissions rates decreased 3%, a relatively small improvement.[10] Its sales of gas-guzzling SUVs such as the Sequoia and full-size pick-up trucks such as the Tundra actually rose as a percentage of its total vehicle sales. According to Toyota insiders,[11] selling more SUVs and trucks is a pragmatic response to a market opportunity in the short term that also provides a means to fund long-term growth. Part of the company's long-term growth strategy involves moving into environmentally responsible technologies including hydrogen-powered internal combustion engines and fuel cell vehicles.

The Prius, its first major foray into new clean technologies, became a surprising success with nearly 200,000 units sold worldwide in 2006. (The company's 2007 sales target for all hybrids is 430,000.[12]) The Prius hybrid drivetrain increases gas mileage and reduces emissions. At the same time, it reduces operating costs for the owner (especially at higher gasoline prices), while sacrificing little in performance or styling. The car has created a small but growing cadre of passionately supportive customers, and added an environmental and innovative cachet to the Toyota brand's aura of superior quality. If gasoline prices continue to rise, Toyota will have a real advantage in the market as it extends hybrid drivetrains to its complete range of new vehicles. In 2007 Toyota's vice president of powertrain development, Masatami Takimoto, said that the company would convert its entire fleet to hybrid drivetrains by 2020.[13]

As global climate change creates increased pressure for reduced use of fossil fuel, Toyota's advantage will increase further. In addition to creating a competitive advantage in hybrid technology (which Toyota is already licensing to other car makers such as Ford and Nissan), the knowledge and experience Toyota has gained with the electric portion of the hybrid drivetrain also positions it to be a leader in fuel cell electric vehicles as that technology matures.

The reframing of value creation at Toyota does not focus on stakeholder issues as ends in themselves. The purpose is not to pursue social and environmental causes independent of economic payback. Such would be the case if the company operated only in terms of stakeholder value. Instead, reframing value creation serves to implement an integrated approach to more significant and sustained benefits for a company whose goal is to remain a global industry leader in the decades ahead.

If you want a friend, get a dog

Al "Chainsaw" Dunlap notoriously repudiated the rights of stakeholders, adding: "You are not in business to be liked . . . If you want a friend get a dog. I'm not taking chances; I have two dogs."[14]

Despite such views still prevalent in companies, in the minds of many business leaders, stakeholders have gone from having illegitimate claims on business value to having a limited voice primarily focused on ensuring compliance, to now being value-creating partners with whom the company can collaborate for mutual benefit. Today's mind-set in business is hardly uniform, but it is changing.

The underlying reasons for such evolving perceptions of stakeholders are rooted in the new competitive landscape.

Ann Svendsen, author of *The Stakeholder Strategy: Profiting from Collaborative Business Relationship*,[15] argues that 60% of corporate value is tied to such intangible assets as reputation, goodwill, employee know-how, and stakeholder trust. Her research corroborates the findings of Baruch Lev, in the work cited earlier,[16] that intangibles now constitute 70% or more of a company's stock price. Whatever the exact number, there is consensus that intangibles are a growing part of market capitalization and longevity.[17] According to Svendsen: "Research now shows that companies that treat their employees, customers, suppliers and communities well are twice as likely to be around in the long term."

Ann Svendsen makes a useful distinction between "stakeholder management" and "stakeholder collaboration." In the former type of relationship (fragmented, ad hoc, linked to short-term business goals, and focused on controlling outcomes), companies appear more business-focused yet paradoxically create lower value from their stakeholder engagements. They manage stakeholders in a hierarchical control model in which relative power determines whether the company or its stakeholders achieve their respective aims when one wins and the other typically loses. In this light, Monsanto's attempt in the late 1990s to limit how (and when) farmers could use its genetically modified corn and Roundup Ready® soybean seeds could be seen as a failed attempt to manage consumer and environmental impacts by tightly controlling the outcomes. This is not the view of stakeholders or of their relationship to a company implied in the sustainable value model.

In the sustainable value model, the focus is on building relationships and on creating opportunities for mutual benefits linked to long-term business goals. In collaborative stakeholder relations, there is an explicit coherence among economic, social, and environmental objectives that leads to business innovations that might not otherwise have occurred.

The leadership challenge

Stakeholder value is often poorly managed in companies that are otherwise global industry leaders. Several factors contribute to this situation. An incomplete awareness exists about the company's impacts on stakeholders and how these impacts might in turn affect future business value. Responsibility for social and environmental issues are typically fragmented across the organization and often delegated to those outside the core management team. Finally, line managers are naturally focused on short-term drivers of shareholder value and view stakeholder-related issues as a distraction from their business objectives.

These factors are usually symptoms of what is the most critical barrier to effectively managing stakeholder value—our mental models. A new leadership mind-set is needed to capture the systemic interrelationships between a company and its societal context. In this mind-set, the goal is not only competing with industry rivals, but also meeting the changing expectations of an ever-growing and diverse set of stakeholders.

Capturing sustainable value requires the CEO and leaders with profit and loss (P&L) responsibility to see stakeholder value as essential to the growth of their companies. The primary barrier to adopting a stakeholder perspective stems from the leader's mind-set, not from whether there is business value to be found. Mind-set can be understood as the hidden set of beliefs about the individual, others, and the world. Much as computer operating systems allow only certain software applications to run, our mind-sets dictate the range of possibilities we draw on to solve problems.[18] For instance, if an executive believes that an NGO's primary commitment is to put her company out of business, the actions that occur to her to engage with them will be very different than if she believes that they are both committed to solving a common problem.

Historically, the mind-set required to rise to the top of a large corporation has run counter to adopting a stakeholder perspective in the process of value creation. Executives have tended to focus narrowly on maximizing shareholder value. They have privileged activities that, often unintentionally, externalize negative social and environmental impacts. They have risen to their positions of power precisely because they are able to create shareholder value by maximizing "efficiencies" that legally drive externalities elsewhere.

The idea that maximizing the value of *all* key stakeholders is of interest (much less essential) for business success is quite heretical to what has made leaders successful in the past. Yet stakeholder power is now a reality in the new global business environment. Business leaders who fail to adopt a new mind-set risk putting their companies and careers at risk. In Table 9.1, key aspects of the new mind-set are compared and contrasted to the old mind-set prevailing in many companies today.

There are two powerful motivators for leadership to integrate a stakeholder perspective in everything the company does. The first is **pain**, which is often the primary attention getter. DuPont mobilized its sustainability efforts in 1988 after Greenpeace activists scaled the wall of one

Old mind-set about stakeholder value	New mind-set about stakeholder value
It's not a core business issue	It's part of the core business target
It's a cost center	It's a source of innovation, profit and growth
It's limited to incremental change (minor cost reductions or product extensions)	It's about breakthrough change and game-changing moves
It's a project for EHS specialists	"I own it"
I'm a victim (of the media, of NGOs, etc.)	I'm responsible for stakeholder perceptions
I'll deal with it if I'm forced	I choose it because I see its value
It's us versus them (company versus stakeholders)	It's us *and* them
Not part of short-term financial results	Paybacks can be under a year; both near- and long-term results are needed
It's an issue-by-issue problem	It's a whole-system opportunity

TABLE 9.1 **The "old" versus "new" leadership**

of its plants and hung a giant banner "DuPont Number One Polluter" facing a highway used by thousands of commuters. DuPont CEO Chad Holliday recalls that event as the spark that led the company to clean up its act. The 1995 Brent Spar media circus that followed Shell's failed attempt to dispose of an oil platform in the North Sea was a similar wake-up call for its senior management.

The second motivator is a compelling **vision** that encompasses the company's societal contribution. Companies with CEOs who have personally espoused a vision for sustainability include Ray Anderson at Interface, Patrick Cescau at Unilever, and Rick George at Suncor.

In other cases, a stakeholder mind-set arises out of the company's culture and historic way of conducting business. Toyota's passionate focus on efficiency and getting rid of waste (*Muda*) allowed it to adopt environmental sustainability as a natural extension of its existing business mind-set. By building on what is best in a company's existing culture and business model, the risk of slow adoption or rejection is lowered.

Leaders who prove adept at mobilizing their organizations play to people's emotions as well as intellect. A stakeholder value mind-set requires an ability to connect to others and to be empathetic. Perceptions of accountability, trust, and reputation stem from the company's ability to live its values. Companies such as SC Johnson, Timberland, and Novo Nordisk have cultures that successfully emphasize strong employee–stakeholder relationships in the field. Enron, with its intellectual commitment to ethics but failed ability to live them, is the perfect anti-example. At some level, Enron and other examples like it are failures to connect emotionally to the world around them.

The stakeholder management process described in the next section is contingent on leadership that is willing and able to alter the dominant mental model of the organization. It is not necessary for every single employee to buy into a stakeholder view, but the risk of failure is significantly elevated if the CEO and key senior executives do not actively promote it.

Creating sustainable value requires specific financial, strategic, and measurement competencies to integrate stakeholder impacts into the value delivery capability of a company. Based on the experiences of global industry leaders that have adopted the sustainable value approach, these competencies fall into the eight disciplines described in Chapter 10. The following toolkit is structured to help companies excel at sustainable value creation. The eight disciplines can also easily be fitted to change-management processes designed to help companies deal with discontinuous change. In Chapter 11, the eight disciplines are reframed in terms of change management for large complex organizations.

10

The eight disciplines

Leading companies are finding that new strategic and organizational skills are required to integrate stakeholder considerations into the value delivery capability of their organizations. Sophisticated managerial competencies now exist to manage shareholder value, from valuing investment opportunities using Economic Value Added (EVA), to assessing changing customer preferences using multi-dimensional maps based on composite product attributes. However, the competencies to manage stakeholder value in a way that integrates environmental and social issues into core business decisions remain unfamiliar territory in all but a handful of companies.

Table 10.1 summarizes the eight disciplines that form the core competencies required to create sustainable value. All eight are essential to achieving the goal and must be considered as parts of a whole process. The eight disciplines are integrated into a management process that executives can use in their organizations to discover and create sustainable value in a step-by-step approach. Six disciplines are organized into two sub-processes ("discover value opportunities" and "create value") with the seventh discipline serving as a feedback loop from one sub-process to the other. The eighth is a meta-discipline designed to increase the organization's capacity to deliver sustainable value over time.

Mastery of these eight disciplines is critical to succeeding in the new stakeholder-rich competitive environment.

Discipline	Key attributes
1 Understand current value position	Understand where and how the company is creating or destroying *stakeholder* value—and what it means in terms of business risks and opportunities
2 Anticipate future expectations	Track emerging issues and interests for stakeholders—and what it means for future business risks and opportunities
3 Set sustainable value goals	Establish a strategic intent to create new business value based on reducing negative impacts and/or increasing positive impacts for key stakeholders
4 Design value creation initiatives	Identify value creation opportunities that elevate both financial and societal performance
5 Develop the business case	Build a compelling business case. Obtain the resources and support needed to move the value creation initiatives forward
6 Capture the value	Assess the requirements to successfully implement the initiatives
7 Validate results and capture learning	Measure progress. Develop metrics for stakeholder value and how it translates into shareholder value
8 Build sustainable value organizational capacity	Develop the mind-set, management capabilities, and skills needed to capture shareholder and stakeholder value

TABLE 10.1 **The eight disciplines of sustainable value**

Source: Adapted from *The Sustainable Company* by Chris Laszlo. Copyright © 2005 by the author. Reproduced by permission of Island Press, Washington, D.C.

The competencies needed to *identify* sustainable value opportunities and those required to *execute* actions to capture those opportunities are very different. Many companies have one set or the other but not both. A gap in either of these areas will thwart the intended result. Disciplines 7 and 8 are accelerators in the process of sustainable value creation; they can make the difference between a company that has occasional successes in this area and a company that is a consistent leader.

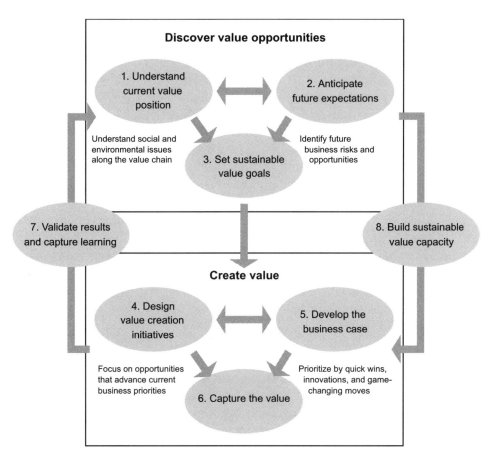

The eight disciplines

1. Establish a baseline value assessment of existing business activities, including the value created or destroyed for key stakeholders.
2. Create a shared vision of future stakeholder expectations and what this means in terms of business opportunities and risks.
3. Set a strategic intent and define targets for creating shareholder value while reducing negative impacts and/or creating value for stakeholders.
4. Design sustainable value initiatives with direct line-management involvement.
5. Develop a financially rigorous business case for the initiatives that includes the resources required and the estimated return-on-investment.
6. Implement the initiatives to capture the value.
7. Validate the results and capture lessons learned.
8. Throughout the process, build organizational capabilities and skills needed to assess and capture sustainable value.

FIGURE 10.1 The eight disciplines of sustainable value

Source: Adapted from *The Sustainable Company* by Chris Laszlo. Copyright © 2005 by the author. Reproduced by permission of Island Press, Washington, D.C.

Applying the eight disciplines

How leading companies use the eight disciplines varies widely—in some cases, the effort may start with a single initiative led by sustainability champions in one business unit; in other cases, the CEO engages the entire organization, as is the case for Lee Scott at Wal-Mart and Jeffrey Immelt at General Electric. Scale is a much less important predictor of success than the inclusion of all the disciplines and involvement of key stakeholders in a whole-system approach.

Companies can start with any one of the eight disciplines as long as all eight are eventually included.

Consider the example of a chemical manufacturer supplying dyestuffs to the textile industry for coloring cotton and rayon fiber. This company may not have a carefully thought-out plan for creating sustainable value. It may not have or even wish to have a baseline assessment of its existing stakeholder impacts. In fact, it may be defensive about these performance areas, and senior management may oppose any efforts to include stakeholder issues.

Sustainable value creation in this company might begin with the design of a particular value creation initiative (Discipline 4). A company R&D team develops a new molecule that increases quality (higher fixation rates, better color consistency) and lowers environmental impacts for textile customers by reducing their amounts of waste dye and auxiliary chemicals. In early market tests, increased market share and higher margins draw the attention of senior management to new and emerging customer procurement criteria (Discipline 2): textile companies are suddenly buying dyestuff on the basis of price, quality, *and* environmental impacts in response to rocketing wastewater treatment costs. Furthermore, the customers of the chemical company's customers are beginning to purchase finished textile products using environmental and social performance criteria. The company's current position (Discipline 1) is then evaluated relative to the emerging market expectations of environmental and social performance.

With the momentum of a successful initiative that helps to prove the business case (Discipline 5) in a business unit of the company, managers from several areas (marketing, finance, manufacturing) become involved. The early success with an environmentally advantageous dye molecule is followed by further corporate-level efforts that engage the larger organization in developing a sustainable value intent and specific strategic goals for the company as a whole (Discipline 3). A cross-functional "sustainable value championship team" is then charged in partnership with business unit heads with capturing sustainable value (Discipline 6) through additional products and services based on environmental or social attributes. The CFO organization is closely involved in measuring progress and validating results (Discipline 7). Once there are visible financial results, the Board invests in building sustainable value capacity in diverse parts of the organization (Discipline 8). It is at this point that the company and its supply chain partners begin to transform into an economically, socially, and environmentally sustainable system.

The eight disciplines, as a cohesive set of competencies, provide the best and most rigorous chances of success in creating sustainable value. The remainder of the chapter lays out each discipline, showing the key tools required and, in many cases, examples of one or more leading companies applying these tools.

Discipline 1: Understand the current value position

Understanding the current position means being able to determine the value created or destroyed by the company. This requires an assessment of the environmental and social impacts of the business on its stakeholders and an understanding of how those impacts lead to value creation or destruction.

The shareholder/stakeholder value map shown in Figure 9.1 is a central tool in this assessment step. Only companies operating in the upper right quadrant, which deliver value to their shareholders without transferring it from other stakeholders, have a truly sustainable business model. The assessment should include the extent to which existing environmental and social initiatives add value along *both* dimensions. What value do these initiatives create for shareholders *and* stakeholders?

Companies can place their businesses (by product, process, business unit, or geographical area) on this map once they have an understanding of the shareholder and stakeholder dimensions for each case. This map is particularly useful in tracking changes over time and in comparing business options.

Insight into sustainable value

Only when environmental and social initiatives are perceived as value contributors to the business will they be effectively integrated by shareholders.

Only when business initiatives are perceived as value contributors to society will the pursuit of profit be given full support by stakeholders.

The above two conditions happen simultaneously only in the upper right-hand quadrant of Figure 9.1.

Assessing stakeholder impacts

In Discipline 1, managers take into account the environmental, social, and economic impacts of their business on key stakeholders along the value chain. The value chain should include not only those value-added activities performed by the business unit doing the assessment. It should represent the full life-cycle of the product from raw materials to product disposal. This requires knowledge of activities and players that is often missing. Merchandise managers in retail companies, for example, work closely with vendors but have little idea about the value-added activities upstream from the vendor. A merchandise manager for cotton clothing would have little reason to know the value-added activities of cotton farming and the environmental impacts from conventional mono-irrigation with synthetic pesticides and insecticides.

This situation is typical in a broad range of sectors: the stakeholder value created or destroyed by a company's suppliers (or its suppliers' suppliers) may be little understood by the company's managers, while the environmental or social impacts in product use and disposal are seen as the responsibility of customers or the end-users.

The impacts assessment should include those stakeholders that have traditionally been considered adversarial or marginal, but this does not mean trying to please every individual or group—indeed, trade-offs and non-satisfaction of one or more groups are an increasing reality in today's complex business environments.

Figure 10.2 shows the environmental, social, and economic impacts along a full value chain which includes the company's own operations as

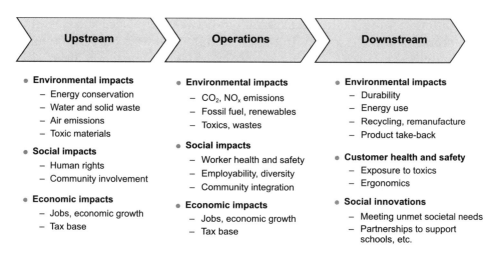

Upstream	Operations	Downstream
• **Environmental impacts**	• **Environmental impacts**	• **Environmental impacts**
– Energy conservation	– CO_2, NO_x emissions	– Durability
– Water and solid waste	– Fossil fuel, renewables	– Energy use
– Air emissions	– Toxics, wastes	– Recycling, remanufacture
– Toxic materials		– Product take-back
• **Social impacts**	• **Social impacts**	
– Human rights	– Worker health and safety	• **Customer health and safety**
– Community involvement	– Employability, diversity	– Exposure to toxics
	– Community integration	– Ergonomics
• **Economic impacts**		• **Social innovations**
– Jobs, economic growth	• **Economic impacts**	– Meeting unmet societal needs
– Tax base	– Jobs, economic growth	– Partnerships to support
	– Tax base	schools, etc.

FIGURE 10.2 Assessing impacts along the value chain

well as the activities of its suppliers (upstream) and customers/end-users (downstream). Discipline 1 requires managers to understand these types of stakeholder impacts along their business unit's full (end-to-end) value chain.

The discipline of assessing stakeholder impacts forces managers to have a new understanding of their product or service life-cycle, which in turn can lead to new insights about their business model and new opportunities for innovation.

To assess impacts along the value chain, managers draw on data from internal management systems. Structured dialogs with stakeholders, such as community advisory panels, can add valuable external perspectives. These sources of information can be tailored to a company's specific environmental and social issues. They provide a baseline for assessing stakeholder impacts along the value chain.

However, these sources are usually not sufficient. To gauge market expectations of stakeholder performance and to determine what may be missing in an internal compliance perspective, leading companies increasingly turn to external stakeholder performance standards which increasingly offer the same rigor and objectivity as financial standards. Like financial standards, they may be subject to interpretation (and to misrepresentation as in the Enron case), but they are converging on a shared set of measures, by industry, of what it means to create or destroy value for stakeholders. It should be noted that there may be significant differences in stakeholder expectations between developed and emerging economies. For example, in the UK, cellphone towers are seen by some activists as destroying value for nearby residents who worry about electro-magnetic frequency (EMF) radiation, while in Africa cellphone towers are seen as a symbol of progress in a context where economic development is far more important than what may be considered to be a secondary health impact.

The main sources of external performance indicators of stakeholder value are listed below:

- Global reporting frameworks and performance standards such as the Global Reporting Initiative[1] and the UN Global Compact[2] to which major global companies (and increasingly small and medium-sized companies) have become signatories

- Sustainability metrics from the capital markets, developed by asset managers such as SAM Group and socially responsible investment (SRI) rating agencies such as Innovest in the United States and Vigeo in France and Belgium

- Industry measures such as those produced by the Global Environmental Management Initiative (GEMI), the American Chemistry Council and its Responsible Care program, and the Sustainable Forestry Initiative (SFI)

These external sources provide measures of environmental and social performance or, in some cases such as the UN Global Compact, the principles and guidelines by which measures can be designed, as well as a degree of objectivity that is often missing in internal management systems or direct dialog with stakeholder groups.

SRI rating agencies have been particularly effective at developing stakeholder criteria that correlate with shareholder value, based on their need to serve fund managers and others in the financial community. The Innovest performance measures, for example, are designed with no overt social and environmental advocacy, no bias from any one individual or company, and a low likelihood of any single NGO overly influencing the metrics used. Innovest employs sophisticated econometric modeling to determine which environmental and sustainability measures are statistically correlated with financial performance. With hundreds of performance measures tailored for each sector it studies, Innovest provides a much-needed degree of objectivity and specificity to stakeholder value. In the automobile sector, for example, Innovest evaluates the major automobile manufacturers using indicators such as Corporate Average Fuel

Economy (CAFE) standards, percentage cars versus light trucks, recyclability of the vehicles, ISO 14001 compliance, product safety, materials efficiency, the number of hybrid and fuel cell projects, and whether the company uses environmental performance factors in compensating its executives.

Of course, these external standards can (and should) be used in concert with one or more internal systems of performance measurement. The challenge for companies is to develop a balanced process for determining what is important for their stakeholders in ways that also make sense for their business. There is no one-size-fits-all approach, and stakeholder value is therefore best assessed using a tailored set of measures that fit the company's unique business situation and circumstances.

Here are some of the aspects to look for in assessing stakeholder impacts:

1. Severity of impacts
   - Degree of damage by environmental category (water, air, soil, natural resources, climate change, biodiversity)
   - Harm by social category (labor conditions, fair wages, local communities, human rights)
   - Perceived injury by stakeholder groups (customers, suppliers, business partners)

2. Location of impacts
   - Where along the extended value chain are the impacts?
   - Where along the value chain are the players responsible for the impacts (raw materials extractor, supplier, manufacturer, distributor, end-user)?

3. Implications of impacts
   - Business (fines, costs, reputation, lost market share, regulation)
   - Perceived ethical standards

4. Causes of impacts (policies, practices, process design, product design, inputs, product end-of-life)

In determining the severity of stakeholder impacts, it is valuable for companies to consider the impacts of their products and activities by *absolute standards* and *relative to peers*. Absolute standards are those that meet science-based tests for stakeholder well-being. For example, in the case of cellphones, the ANSI/IEEE[3] radiowave frequency exposure standard for the general public is 0.57 mW/cm² (milliwatts per square centimeter).

The standard is based on extensive scientific research into the biological effect of radiowave absorption on humans. Relative standards are those that compare stakeholder value created or destroyed by the company, relative to other companies in the same sector. Cellphone manufacturers offer some handset models that have lower radio frequency emissions than others.

Companies in the metal smelting and electroplating industries produce heavy metal by-products that are highly toxic to human cells. These companies are unlikely to create anything but negative environmental impacts by the absolute standards of sustainability, but an individual company's performance can be far superior to the electroplating industry average through the use of closed-loop processes and excellence in waste remediation practices. When stakeholder impacts are insufficient in an absolute sense but superior to those of the company's peers, they can translate into additional shareholder value because of their relative performance advantage.

Carrying out an effective stakeholder value assessment should result in the identification of stakeholder issues and a better understanding of how the company impacts those stakeholder issues and interests.

The example matrix presented in Table 10.2 is a useful tool for this assessment. Executives can use the matrix to answer three key questions, corresponding to the table's three columns:

1. Who are our most important stakeholders?

2. What are each stakeholder group's unique interests and issues in relation to our business activities?

3. How do we affect this stakeholder group and in particular where do we currently destroy value for it?

Readers can fill in the matrix for their businesses.

Challenges

- Stakeholder value is more complex to measure than shareholder value. It requires the ability to assess perceptions and to deal with high emotional content. Dialog can evolve the assessment and reduce the emotional content

- Some stakeholder groups may hold positions that conflict with those of other stakeholders. Managers need to accept that one or more stakeholder groups may always be dissatisfied with what the company is doing

Stakeholders	Issues and interests	Manufacturers' impacts on stakeholder issues and interests
PC and cellphone customers	• Desire to have the latest product versus concern about environment	*Value destruction by manufacturers*: • Current offers require a trade-off for customers: either get the latest product *or* be environmentally responsible • No product offering that allows users to meet both needs simultaneously
NGOs, e.g. the Silicon Valley Toxics Coalition	• Use of non-renewable and toxic raw materials in electronic equipment • Growth of e-waste • Desire to see re-use in low-income communities	*Value destruction by manufacturers*: • Toxic materials still used (non-compliance with RoHS) • Lack of systematic recycle and re-use policies • Products not designed for long life or re-use
Local communities	• Clean and healthy environment (air, water, soil) • Access to low-cost refurbished products in low-income communities	*Value destruction by manufacturers*: • Toxic equipment in landfills; soil and water contamination • Lack of systematic outreach to low-income markets
Regulators and government	• Compliance with standards such as WEEE and RoHS • Active protection of the environment and re-use/recycling practices	*Value destruction by manufacturers*: • Non-compliance outside US/European markets • Lack of partnership with regulators to encourage re-use/recycling practices
Employees of PC and cellphone manufacturers	• Brand image • Demotivation from sense of contributing to environmental harm • Desire to work for employer-of-choice	*Value destruction by manufacturers*: • CSR policies of the firm don't address real issues • Companies don't walk the talk

CSR = corporate social responsibility; RoHS = Restriction of Hazardous Substances; WEEE = waste electrical and electronic equipment

TABLE 10.2 **Example matrix of stakeholder issues/impacts—recycling and re-using personal computers and cellphone handsets**

- Managers need to be able to work with stakeholders who are critical of the company as long as those groups are willing to be constructive. Stakeholders who operate in bad faith or who are only interested in harming the company should be avoided after the company has made its own best-faith effort to engage them in finding common ground

- Creating internal commitment to the concept of stakeholder value, and a willingness to invest senior management time and energy to learn how to assess stakeholder value

- Keeping the analysis at the appropriate level of detail—deep enough to provide relevance and insight but not so detailed as to cause endless debate or a loss of strategic perspective

- Using the right measures—ones that are relevant to the industry and to its key stakeholders yet reflect emerging performance standards such as those implicit in the Global Reporting Initiative and Innovest metrics

- Segmenting stakeholder groups, linking stakeholder segments to the impacts, and then identifying those segments that require the most attention

- Assessing stakeholder value using both absolute standards and those that measure performance relative to peers

Discipline 2: Anticipate future expectations

Discipline 2 assesses the probable future expectations of stakeholders. It takes the baseline view of shareholder/stakeholder value created in Discipline 1 and asks: "What might change?" The purpose is to understand how stakeholder expectations may evolve and what this means in terms of business opportunities and risks.

The rapidly evolving debate on climate change has created new expectations that companies will no longer be able to dump carbon in the atmosphere for free. These expectations in turn create business risks for companies with carbon-intensive investments. The scrapping of TXU's coal-fired power plants in early 2007 is a case in point. A carbon-constrained world also offers huge business opportunities for those companies that offer low carbon-intensity products and services. General Electric's "ecomagination" strategy is a clear example of the latter.

"What-if" scenarios with quantified stakeholder impacts help to ready an organization for change. As described in my earlier book, *Large Scale Organizational Change:*[4]

> What-if scenarios are not undertaken as an exercise in prediction; they are part of creating a mind-set that is open to radical change. If you are asking yourself what your company would do in case its future proves radically different from the past, it is probably already too late. Companies must integrate into their strategies a number of scenarios for radically alternative futures. Such envisioning of the future can remain fact based and issue driven, even if it represents a discontinuity with the past and present . . . The syndrome of compiling quarterly reports and annual budgets can be extremely limiting to a company's ability to adapt to fundamental change. Although these short-term exercises are efficient and necessary for a host of reasons, they must not allow senior management to privilege the short term at the cost of sustainability by optimizing existing structures and processes in a world in which these structures and processes are becoming irrelevant.

Leading companies develop a process for managing stakeholder expectations and emerging issues to create strategic opportunities for their business. They include feedback from stakeholders through a variety of networks and channels, as well as a regular scanning of emerging issues that are used to challenge assumptions in each business unit. To anticipate threats and opportunities, high-impact event scenarios should be considered. The following two types of high-impact event scenarios are often neglected in favor of the (usually preferred) high-probability, short-term ones.

1. **High-probability, long-term scenarios** drive thinking about major strategic shifts that demand deep changes in a company's capabilities. The automobile industry's look at the stakeholder issues surrounding the internal combustion engine 20 years into the future is such a scenario. In the face of such a long-term but likely future, an auto manufacturer that identifies its core competence with the fossil-fuel internal combustion engine is increasingly at risk. The investments required to shift to a new

design are immense and cannot be made overnight. The cell-phone industry faces an explosion of demand in emerging markets such as China and India, with as many as one billion new handsets projected in these markets by 2010. What will be the impact in terms of raw materials consumption and e-waste at current rates of churn with consumers seeking to replace their models every 12–18 months? Few companies are good at assessing such scenarios when it comes to environmental and social factors, preferring to extend CSR-type thinking about social responsibility in a framework of incremental change. The risks to shareholder value for the late movers, and the potential opportunities for early movers, become clear through the exercise of this discipline

2. **Low-probability, short-term scenarios** are also important to consider in anticipating future expectations. For a company with CO_2-intensive activities, a sudden dramatic shift in carbon costs (to, say, $100 per ton) or in the regulatory environment (such as a mandatory US federal cap-and-trade policy) related to climate change is such a scenario. A review of the potential risks and opportunities of this scenario might lead the company to take real options on research into alternative processes and products that are less CO_2-intensive, in order to be positioned to sustain shareholder value in the event of a more costly and tightly regulated carbon-constrained world

The key steps in the scenario process are:

- Agree to relevant scenarios using both issue LCA and issue vulnerability analysis. This forces managers to take a system-wide view of emerging trends, looking both up- and downstream at evolving stakeholder expectations

- Assess how future expectations will differ from current expectations for each key stakeholder under each scenario

- Determine the business implications of current and emerging issues. Use the matrix of stakeholder issues/impacts from Discipline 1 (see Table 10.2) to assess the change

- Identify and rank the emerging business opportunities and threats

Mapping Disciplines 1 and 2

Many companies whose core business has historically created value for stakeholders are finding that rising societal expectations lead over time to a situation of stakeholder value destruction—even though the company has made little or no changes to its products. Cigarettes are an obvious example: largely unchanged since the 1950s when they were seen as a legitimate source of pleasure, cigarettes today are facing a worldwide ban from public health stakeholders who support the World Health Organization's Tobacco-Free Initiative. The specific circumstances surrounding tobacco mirror a larger phenomenon affecting businesses in every sector: a greater fear of health risks combined with a higher standard for what is deemed acceptable in terms of the unintended consequences of business on human health and the environment.

A leading car company like Toyota sees its stakeholder value as positive today, but risks being seen as negative in the future if fossil-fuel internal combustion engines continue their damage to the global climate, air quality, and resource depletion. Figure 10.3 shows the sustainable value trend for Toyota.

The same pattern of rising stakeholder expectations, with a drift to the left in the stakeholder/shareholder map shown in Figure 10.3, is true for

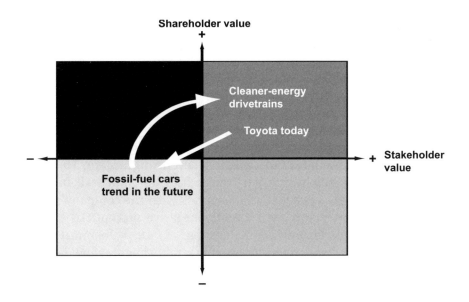

FIGURE 10.3 Anticipating future expectations for Toyota

makers of children's toys, cosmetics, household cleaning products, project finance, property and casualty insurance, and many other sectors.

In other cases, companies begin with a profitable business that destroys stakeholder value (they are operating in the upper left-hand quadrant of Figure 9.1). These companies have the opportunity to redesign their products or processes to create stakeholder value in a way that contributes to their competitive advantage. Lafarge, the world's second largest aggregates producer with over 700 quarries, created a partnership in 2001 with the World Wildlife Fund (WWF) to restore its spent quarries beyond compliance levels. Doing so created value for local communities and the environment, while producing significant business benefits for Lafarge.

Still other companies are starting new businesses based explicitly on environmental or social benefits. Cargill's NatureWorks® meets the need for biodegradable packaging derived from plant materials to replace energy-intensive plastics derived from non-renewable petroleum products. In terms of Figure 9.1, these companies begin in the center of the shareholder/stakeholder map, with a proposal for a new business unit that does not as yet exist. If successful, the new business will offer environmental and social benefits in a way that creates shareholder value, moving the business unit into the upper right-hand quadrant of the shareholder/stakeholder map.

The outcome of Discipline 2 is a strategic vision of value opportunities as well as a set of prioritized emerging issues and their implications for the business. The greatest potential for sustainable value creation lies in going beyond the known solution set. Engaging stakeholders can unlock hidden value and generate otherwise missed opportunities (new materials, processes, products, markets, rules of the game).

Challenges

- A frequent fear of line managers is that engaging with societal stakeholders will lead to a public relations nightmare. The concern is that soliciting input from critics, or from stakeholders who hold perspectives that are at odds with the company's narrow business views, will amplify negative perceptions of the company. Yet leading companies such as Dow Chemical with high negative risks have successfully established stakeholder dialog forums in order to better understand future expectations. Doing so has, if anything, decreased stakeholder resistance, rather than increasing it as they initially feared it would

- Thinking outside the box and not just extrapolating trends from the past. Incremental efforts to improve social and environmental performance are frequently inadequate in the face of complex stakeholder issues such as climate change, water scarcity, and global poverty. In many cases, companies addressing future sustainability challenges need to have the courage and imagination to undertake breakthrough thinking, even if it may lead to redesigning their core business models

- Avoiding the tendency to see the company's impacts in a fragmented and unsystematic way; seeing the complex interrelationships and potential reinforcing or feedback loops that can create risks or opportunities

- Remaining practical and advancing business priorities rather than pursuing social and environmental causes for their own sake

- Deep listening of external stakeholders using a broad range of information sources about emerging issues

- Creating strategically meaningful scenarios with quantified stakeholder impacts

- Including low-probability short-term events and high-probability long-term events where the outcomes may be significant to the business

Discipline 3: Set sustainable value goals

Discipline 3 establishes a target of creating additional value for shareholders by reducing negative stakeholder impacts and/or creating value for them. New business objectives are developed using a stakeholder lens along the full value chain. New product and process designs are identified based on creating stakeholder value (or on reducing stakeholder value destruction). Business opportunities are then turned into actions that demonstrate desired results that in turn build momentum to achieve additional sustainable value goals.

At the heart of this inquiry-driven process is greater awareness of the business possibilities for improving environmental and social performance throughout the value chain. Such an inquiry requires a creative vision for profitably meeting the needs of customers while creating societal benefits. New value can be created in many ways including:

- Better management of risks and reputation

- Reduction of energy costs and materials waste

- Redesign of products to serve customers better while reducing negative impacts on human health and the environment (or while offering new health and environmental benefits)

- Development of new businesses that contribute to improving social and environmental well-being, such as meeting unmet nutritional or health needs in emerging markets

- A brand identity built around contributing to society

There are two key tools in this discipline. The first is the sustainable value intent. Like the strategic intent used in classic visioning exercises for discontinuous change, the sustainable value intent gives voice to the aspirations of the company's leadership. It can be CEO-led or it can be generated by sustainable value champions throughout the organization.[5] Here the resulting intent integrates stakeholder value into the vision of a desirable future for the business. The second tool is the six levels of strategic focus. It helps a company to identify where business value can be created from the actions that support the strategic intent. The six levels of value creation is a tool that offers managers a broader view of strategic options than is usually the case with environmental or social initiatives. These two tools are described below.

The sustainable value intent

The sustainable value intent is a statement that is widely adopted throughout the organization. It expresses a particular desirable future that the company is committed to achieving. It combines superior shareholder value with stakeholder value. Like a traditional strategic intent, it sets ambitions greater than means. It aims for targets that it doesn't necessarily know how to achieve given current capabilities. These targets guide everything the company does.

The strategic intent with its backcasting methodology is particularly effective in organizations committed to sustainability because of its role in creating discontinuous change: it allows executives to design a future state that is informed by the past but is not an extension of it. By their very nature, many of the underlying sustainability issues such as climate change and global poverty demand radical solutions from the planet and society's perspective. By failing to address these issues in a meaningful way, companies may not only be missing the opportunity to make a difference to society; they may be missing huge business opportunities. A coal-based power company that sees its future only in terms of cleaner coal (in other words, incremental improvements to existing technology) may be putting its business future at risk compared to an electric utility that sets its sights on zero emissions fuels and renewables with distributed generation and storage infrastructure.

The outcome of the sustainable value intent is an aligned set of key decision-makers inside and outside the company. Whatever the circumstances of the company and its sector, an intent focused on sustainable value creation must include key stakeholder voices capable of representing the whole system.

DuPont is an example of a company that was widely seen as an environmental offender ten years ago, yet has developed a strong strategic intent to serve its shareholders and the planet in a mutually reinforcing way, expressed in its new mission "to be the world's most dynamic science company, creating sustainable solutions essential to a better, safer and healthier life for people everywhere" (see Chapter 5). The company has succeeded in involving a diverse range of stakeholders in the elaboration of its strategic intent.

In practice, the sustainable value intent often has three key components:

- **Vision.** A one-sentence declaration of an extraordinary future that the company is committed to achieving. "We, the people of DuPont, dedicate ourselves daily to the work of improving life on our planet"

- **Values.** The shared principles and behaviors that guide how the company intends to conduct itself in pursuit of its vision; DuPont's principles state: "We will respect nature and living things, work safely, be gracious to one another and our partners, and each day we will leave for home with consciences clear and spirits soaring"

- **Strategic objectives.** The concrete business goals that will allow the company to realize its vision and values; DuPont's sustainable value goals include the following four goals for 2010, supplementing existing financial goals:

  a. To derive 25% of revenues from non-depletable resources, up from 14% in 2002

   b. To reduce global carbon-equivalent greenhouse gas emissions by 65%, using 1990 as the base year (the company has already surpassed this goal with a 72% reduction)

   c. To hold energy use flat, using 1990 as the base year (currently the company has reduced global energy use 7% below 1990 levels)

   d. To source 10% of the company's global energy use in the year 2010 from renewable resources (the company has now reached 5%)

Whole-system change

For a company facing business issues involving multiple stakeholders in diverse markets, the conventional approach to coming up with its vision, values, and strategic objectives is grossly inadequate. Why should managers establish a strategic intent with an approach based on a small insular management team holding relatively homogenous views?

An alternative approach to setting a strategic intent is a whole-system approach such as is used in Appreciative Inquiry, a strength-based approach to scaling change. While still in its infancy as an approach to creating sustainable value, Appreciative Inquiry has been successfully used by many companies facing sustainability challenges.[6] Appreciative Inquiry allows participants to discover the best of their shared experiences and tap into the larger system's capacity for cooperation. Efforts to discover and elaborate the positive core (the past, present, and future capacities of the whole system) lead to a vision, values, and strategic objectives that integrate societal stakeholder issues which are often excluded from consideration in conventional approaches. According to J. Ludema,[7] having the whole system involved in the process generates an ecological perspective in which:

> . . . all the pieces of the puzzle come together in one place and everyone can gain an appreciation for the whole. The unique perspective of each person, when combined with the perspectives of others, creates new possibilities for action, possibilities that previously lay dormant or undiscovered.

In this way Appreciative Inquiry enables participants to stand open to possibilities that might otherwise escape notice.

These distinctive characteristics make Appreciative Inquiry a collaborative effort to discover what is healthy, successful, and positive in business organizations as they are embedded in their human and natural environments. Appreciative Inquiry enables the discovery of new possibilities when the whole system is operating at its best. It uncovers organizational strengths and competencies that contribute to exceptional performance and vitality. It is the most effective way for companies to establish a robust strategic intent that incorporates shareholder and stakeholder value.

The six levels of strategic focus

The six levels of strategic focus shown in Figure 10.4 constitute an important tool for identifying value creation. Here the six levels are presented in general terms as they apply to virtually every company.

Many companies have made great strides in risk mitigation (level 1) and process cost reduction (level 2) through eliminating waste and improving energy efficiencies. Relatively few have focused on top-line growth based on product or brand differentiation (levels 3 and 5). Even fewer have used stakeholder value creation as a way to drive new markets and business context change (levels 4 and 6).

FIGURE 10.4 **The six levels of strategic focus**

Source: From *The Sustainable Company* by Chris Laszlo. Copyright © 2005 by the author. Reproduced by permission of Island Press, Washington, D.C.

The number of cases of green products and sustainability brand differentiation is growing steadily. They are entering the business mainstream (and are no longer the exclusive purview of specialty eco-stores such as The Body Shop) as illustrated by organic cotton baby clothes such as the Baby George line sold at "every day low prices" in Wal-Mart stores. Green product and brand differentiation exist in a wide range of applications including the following:

- Industrial business-to-business products such as lighter, cleaner jet engines (the GEnx line) sold by General Electric with aircraft manufacturers to the airlines

- Consumer products such as the healthy foods, homecare, and personal care products sold under the Unilever brands

- Financial services such as full-service banking that screens loan applicants based on social and environmental performance

In Discipline 3, getting organizational buy-in for sustainable value targets depends on being able to put forward a clear vision of the business value at stake. If the company has done an effective job of assessing existing stakeholder impacts (Discipline 1) and future expectations (Discipline 2), the company may know that it needs to shift strategically. It may even have formulated its target as a sustainable value intent expressed in terms of increased shareholder and stakeholder value. But, unless it has articulated how the proposed target will create business value, it will fail to engage the line managers who ultimately will be accountable for implementation.

Some practical considerations

Practical steps for creating the sustainable value intent, and for identifying where business value can be created by the actions that support the intent, include the following:

1. **Grounding in business value.** The context for integrating the environmental and social dimensions of business activities along the value chain has to be driven by business logic. Is the proposed target a smart business move? Managers understand that sustainability is about advancing existing business priorities and creating new sources of business value

2. **Brainstorming.** How would our company look in an extraordinary future? How would that future be perceived by our shareholders and our key stakeholders?

3. **Criteria selection.** What criteria will we use to evaluate, prioritize, and select the shortlist of targets? Select five to eight key benchmarks specific to the company including those that represent criteria used by societal stakeholders such as NGOs or the media

4. **Synthesis and alignment on the sustainable value targets**
    a. Work in self-selected groups on prioritizing the targets, with cross-sectional representation and external stakeholders to reflect the voices of the whole system in the selection process
    b. Vote on formulating the sustainable value intent and the choice of the sustainable value targets
    c. Create alignment and recommendations to pass on to senior leadership

Discipline 3 is about developing a vision with specific targets to improve shareholder and stakeholder value. It draws on the stakeholder impact assessment of Discipline 1 and the understanding of emerging issues of Discipline 2 to map out value enhancement opportunities using both shareholder and stakeholder dimensions. These opportunities occur at the multiple levels of value creation described in Figure 10.4 and include:

- Risk mitigation
- Process improvement
- Product redesign
- New markets
- Enhanced brand reputation
- A more favorable business context

The targets should typically begin with near-term value improvement (the "quick wins") to gain adherence and buy-in from line managers and financial executives who may be skeptical or who may consider performance targets involving stakeholders to be a low priority. The targets should be fixed in collaboration with line management (through cross-functional guiding coalitions or steering teams) so as not to be seen as technical environmental, health, and safety (EH&S) matters that somehow lie outside the core business. Finally, external stakeholders who can represent the whole system are critical to gaining adherence on environmental and social issues.

The resulting targets can be mapped using Figure 9.1. Targets that unambiguously improve value for shareholders and stakeholders offer the greatest (and most obvious) business opportunities. They are likely to get rapid buy-in from the rest of the organization. Targets that reduce stakeholder value destruction but do not create any visible improvement in shareholder value are a much harder sell. Getting organizational buy-in for these cases will depend on making the business case that reducing negative stakeholder impacts provides hidden benefits for shareholders. Managers proposing such targets will have to reveal these hidden business benefits and articulate them in financial terms (Discipline 5). Other target cases include business products or activities that offer value creation opportunities for shareholders but not stakeholders; and those that improve stakeholder value but remain unattractive for shareholders.

Challenges

- Getting CEO leadership and support for sustainable value initiatives

- Getting cross-functional, cross-company, and cross-sector cooperation where needed

- Involving the whole system including all key stakeholders along the extended supply chain. The Appreciative Inquiry approach does not require all key stakeholders to be personally present, but it does require that all key voices representing the whole system be incorporated into the goal setting

- Pursuing targets that may not have measurable cash-flow benefits today but either significantly reduce negative stakeholder impacts or create positive stakeholder value that translate into shareholder value in the future

- A willingness to look at a wide range of ways in which business value can be created or destroyed. For example, managers may not be used to thinking about greenhouse gas emissions as a way to differentiate their products or as a growing component of their company's reputation

- Effectively using the insights and information from Disciplines 1 and 2 when formulating the strategic intent and setting the sustainable value targets

Discipline 4: Design value creation initiatives

The purpose of Discipline 4 is to design action initiatives that advance the sustainable value goals established through the previous disciplines. A related goal is to integrate stakeholder perspectives into all existing initiatives such as supply chain optimization efforts.

Companies designing action initiatives benefit from taking the whole-system approach described in Discipline 3. When all the key stakeholders are involved in the design of an initiative, it will have greater organizational buy-in and a wider access to resources.

One particularly effective way to get a whole-system perspective over a compressed time is the stakeholder summit. Using the Appreciative Inquiry (AI) change methodology,[8] these summits are able to engage large groups in whole-system change.[9] They typically involve 60–1,000 or more participants over three to five days. They can include senior executives, line managers, front-line employees, customers, suppliers, NGOs, regulators, and other stakeholders who help represent the whole system. Stakeholder summits can be used to rapidly prototype value creation initiatives with the participation of key stakeholders. For more detail on how whole-system stakeholder summits can lead to the rapid design of sustainable value initiatives, see also Laszlo and Cooperrider, "Design for Sustainable Value: A Whole System Approach."[10]

The output of Discipline 4 is a completed initiative design and implementation plan that has broad support inside and outside the organization.

A key to Discipline 4 is establishing appropriate design criteria so that the initiatives address the six levels of strategic focus and the stakeholder sources of value identified in Discipline 3. Too often, environmental and social initiatives focus only on risk mitigation or process cost reduction. Although these continue to be important sources of value creation for many companies, product differentiation, new markets, brand enhancement, and changing the rules of the game based on stakeholder performance represent a huge business potential that is often left untapped.

The six levels of strategic focus (see Figure 10.4) for designing value creation initiatives are described below with illustrations and examples.

Level 1: Risk mitigation and compliance-oriented management of risks

Actions companies take to comply with government regulations and industry standards (one of the earliest examples being Responsible Care in the chemicals industry) have historically been seen as a financial burden: they are the necessary cost of doing business and of maintaining license to operate. Yet efficient risk mitigation strategies can create significant value to both shareholders and stakeholders. They include:

- The avoidance of penalties and fines

- Reduced legal fees

- Lower insurance premiums and/or product liability costs

- Reduced site remediation costs

- A lower probability of catastrophic events

Level 2: Process cost reductions

Process cost reductions are often one of the first stakeholder-oriented initiatives a company undertakes. Reducing energy consumption, eliminating waste, and minimizing materials intensity are all initiatives that save the company money while reducing environment, health, and safety impacts on stakeholders.

Process cost reductions can be addressed in the framework of existing operational efficiency initiatives such as Six Sigma.[11] They can become an incremental extension of efficient resource use.

Finally, efforts to reduce environmental process costs can provide the context for process innovation and reveal other opportunities for redesigning value-added activities or the products and services offered.

Level 3: Product differentiation to meet new customer needs for social and environmental attributes

The growing segment of consumers for whom social and environmental attributes are important decision criteria provides an opportunity for leading companies to differentiate themselves on a dimension other than price or technical performance. Al Gore's film *An Inconvenient Truth*,[12] along with a changing political awareness of climate change, is helping to push sustainability issues into the forefront of public consciousness. On the supply side of the equation, mainstream players such as Wal-Mart and General Electric are democratizing green products by bringing unit costs in line with the products' traditional (non-green) counterparts. It is now possible to buy an organic V-neck shirt at Wal-Mart for about the same price as one made from conventionally grown cotton.

When consumers are not asked to pay more for environmental and social benefits, and when they are not forced to compromise quality or performance, sustainability attributes become a "plus one." The recent experience of leading companies from Unilever to Toyota, and J.P. Morgan Chase to Aviva, shows that consumers prefer green products and services if they do not have to give up anything in return.

Level 4: Penetrating new markets and developing new businesses based on sustainability

Technological innovation that creates stakeholder value increasingly opens up new markets. Examples include DuPont's push into soy-based nutritional products and Procter & Gamble's development of water purification products in emerging markets. Aviva, one of the world's largest insurance companies, has begun selling life insurance in rural India for households where the disability or death of the principal wage earner can be devastating. Celanese AG has parlayed its expertise in plastic polymers to develop high-temperature membrane electrode assembly (MEA) for fuel cells suitable for use in cars—itself a new market driven by climate change-related concerns. The French materials giant Saint-Gobain is finding new applications for its high-performance materials from particulate filters in diesel cars to solar panel components and windmill tips.

In other cases, developing an expertise in reducing stakeholder impacts or creating stakeholder value can generate a new revenue stream from an existing business. For example, cement companies with high CO_2 emissions today face financial liabilities while CO_2 emission caps, carbon taxes, plant shutdowns, and even asbestos-type class-action lawsuits loom on the horizon. A cement company that is able to reduce its CO_2 emissions more cost-efficiently than others not only reduces these liabilities, it may also have a new market opportunity to sell CO_2 credits.

Level 5: Enhancing corporate reputation and image

DuPont, Wal-Mart, Unilever, General Electric, Alcoa, and many other leading companies are finding that a brand/culture based on creating stakeholder value is rapidly becoming a source of competitive advantage. Among other business benefits, a sustainability image draws in higher-income consumers, attracts and retains talented people, and can ease negotiations with government regulators concerned about industry impacts. It contributes to an image of innovation—in some cases attached to a single product such as Toyota's Prius—that confers reputation benefits to the entire company.

Level 6: Business context—changing the industry "rules of the game"

At this level, companies attempt to shape in their favor the regulations, practices, and rules that govern how business can be conducted. An example is the US Climate Action Partnership, which began by urging President George W. Bush to support mandatory reductions in greenhouse gas emissions and to propose federal reduction targets. Rather than slowing down climate change legislation, these industry leaders are encouraging it. They see their efforts to reduce emissions, reduce energy use, and provide climate change solutions as a source of future comparative advantage in a carbon-constrained world. These companies don't want the price of oil to fall back to $20 a barrel, as they would lose that advantage relative to competitors who are less energy-efficient and who have a higher intensity of greenhouse gas emissions.[13]

A September 2007 *New York Times* article says that "industry officials, consumer groups and regulatory experts all agree there has been a recent surge of requests for new regulations." The article goes on to say that, "For toys and cars, antifreeze and fireworks, popcorn and produce and cigarettes and lightbulbs, . . . industry groups or major manufacturers are calling for federal health, safety and environmental mandates . . . abandoning years of efforts to block such measures . . . to put into statute what had either previously been volunatry consensus standards or industry goals."[14]

Individual companies that obtain an advantage in a particular stakeholder performance category might lobby legislators to impose harsh penalties in that category on the whole industry in anticipation of obtaining a new source of competitive advantage or creating a new barrier to entry.

Influencing the business context is not only about lobbying government. Increasing the overall stakeholder value in an industry can create goodwill for the entire industry. Conversely, negative stakeholder value can shrink the potential market size and reduce the ability of players in the industry to make enduring profits.

Table 10.3 gives examples of sectors in which stakeholder value is seen as being destroyed for reasons often not recognized by the industry leaders, with associated business implications.

Sector	Stakeholder issue	Consequence for industry
Genetically modified organisms (GMOs)	• Fear of negative health impacts, biodiversity losses	• Consumer rejection • Stock price declines for leaders
Wireless communications (cellphones and masts)	• Electromagnetic frequency radiation (EMF) impact on human health	• Masts dismantled in some communities • Risk of future class-action lawsuits
Cosmetics Children's toys	• Use of phthalates • Use in some cases of Bisphenol A and lead	• Image loss • Fines • Lawsuits • Reduced market size
Energy	• Climate change and use of non-renewable fossil fuels	• Government regulation and energy efficiency measures
Tobacco	• Negative health impacts • Perception that industry practices involve deceit and deception	• Risk of banning tobacco, e.g. Tobacco-Free Initiative and high excise taxes
Cars	• Greenhouse gas emissions and use of fossil fuels	• Pre-emptive government regulation • Slower growth
Cotton clothing	• Use of pesticides and insecticides in farming • Human rights in ginning	• Image of "all natural" cotton fabric at risk • Fines

TABLE 10.3 Business sectors shaped by stakeholder issues in selected industries

Defining capability requirements

Once initiatives are selected and clear targets are set, the next step is for the organization to assess the capabilities it will need. These are the collective abilities of the organization necessary to capture and sustain value successfully. They cover a range of functions from product development to operations and marketing, along with corporate services such as human resources, finance, and legal.

Example capabilities required in the design of sustainable value initiatives include the following:

- Customer responsiveness to meet emerging environmental and social expectations

- Green technology integration

- Design for environment

- Community engagement

- Government partnership

- Serving developing markets and meeting the unmet needs of consumers who have been largely excluded from global markets to date

Managers assessing capability requirements need to identify capability surpluses and gaps by mapping current performance against the capabilities required to implement sustainable value initiatives.

The outcome of this step is a prioritized set of capacity gaps that the company needs to close in order to execute the sustainable value initiatives identified in the previous discipline.

Discipline 4 leads to a completed initiative design and implementation plan along with the actions it needs to take to close any significant capacity gaps in the organization. In the next discipline, establishing a rigorous business case for the initiative creates broad organizational support and provides a firm basis for implementation.

Challenges

- Gaining CEO leadership and business unit support for the sustainable value initiatives and for developing the required capabilities to implement them

- Designing and getting buy-in for initiatives that do not have short-term tangible payoffs, such as human rights policies that go beyond minimal compliance requirements

- Getting line management and financial staff to see environmental and social initiatives as contributors to competitive advantage

- Getting the resources or approval for investments for initiatives before making the business case (Discipline 5)—conversely, not being able to make the business case until the value creation initiatives are approved

- For initiatives at the business unit level, reluctance to push for context changes that disrupt the status quo for the industry as a whole

- Cross-functional teaming and sponsorship by an executive steering committee to obtain the organizational buy-in and resources required at this stage

- Involving external stakeholders in the design of the value creation initiatives

- Working at all six levels of strategic focus (not just risk mitigation and cost reduction)

- Assessing the organizational capabilities needed to capture and sustain value successfully

Discipline 5: Develop the business case

Discipline 5 is about building a compelling business case for the selected sustainable value initiatives. Done right, this step enables managers to obtain the resources and organizational support needed to implement sustainability initiatives as they would for any other proposed investment project.

Once the priority initiatives are formulated (Discipline 4), it is time to quantify (where possible) the shareholder returns in each case.

- Project the costs and benefits, considering the timing and complexity of implementation.

- Assign a monetary value to each initiative, including the impact of stakeholder value on shareholder value.

- Obtain input and buy-in from the line managers who will ultimately be accountable for delivering the results.

All drivers of shareholder value need to be considered, not only revenue increases or cost reductions. Other key value drivers of sustainable value initiatives that contribute to shareholder value are shown in Table 10.4. Line managers frequently focus only on operating profitability when assessing sustainability initiatives, leaving other sources of financial value on the table.

Shareholder value driver	Type of financial value created by sustainable value initiatives
Revenues minus costs	Higher operating profitability: for example, from reduced energy and waste
Capital efficiency	Better asset utilization from initiatives that reduce capital intensity. Leads to higher return on net assets
Cost of capital	Lower cost of access to equity and debt owing to reduced stakeholder-related risks
Growth	Multiplier effects from targeting faster-than-average-growth market segments
Real options	Learning investments in cases of environmentally driven disruptive innovations and green technologies
Market confidence	Intangible factors such as goodwill and stakeholder relationships that have a large immediate impact on stock value

TABLE 10.4 Value drivers and the types of financial value created

The business framework for Discipline 5 relies on two tools that work together to quantify the business case for sustainable value initiatives. The first tool is the six levels of strategic focus presented earlier (see Disciplines 3 and 4). The second tool is shareholder value drivers presented in Table 10.4.

Strategic value assessed through real options analysis is a powerful way to account for the foresight of management teams in creating opportunities and managing risks from emerging issues that might threaten shareholder value. In concept, real options are similar to financial options. Financial options are the right to buy a security at a set date in the future (exercise date) for a set price (strike price). On the exercise date, if the security is worth more than the strike price, then the holder of the option will exercise it and purchase the security. If the security is worth less than the strike price, the investor will not purchase the security.

Real options represent R&D programs, strategic plans, and other activities that position a company to take advantage of an opportunity by making additional investments at a future date. The additional investments represent the strike price of the real option. The underlying security is the future cash flow of the new business. The company will make the additional investments on the exercise date if, at that time, it appears that the business will be profitable. If, on the other hand, conditions are such that the business is unlikely to be successful, the company will save itself from having to make an unprofitable investment. Thus, the real option allows a company to manage future uncertainty through:

- Delaying investment until more is known

- Being ready to move quickly when the conditions are right

Just as a financial option has value whether or not it turns out to be "in the money," a real option also contributes to shareholder value even if it is never exercised. The Black–Scholes formula[15] for calculating the value of financial options is also used with real options.

The management team can use real options in a powerful way to pursue the sustainability strategies described above. Given future uncertainties, some investments required to pursue these strategies may not be justifiable using discounted cash flows. Yet ignoring the uncertainties may leave a company vulnerable to future events.

Real options provide a means of economic justification for strategic action as insurance or as a possible source of future competitive advantage.

In particular, real options enable companies to incorporate low-probability, high-impact scenarios in their value assessment, something that is very difficult to do using a pure discounted cash flow approach to valuation. For example, an oil company using real options could develop strategic plans, and justify R&D and exploratory investments in alternative energy to position it to move quickly if global warming turns out to be more severe than anticipated.

Market confidence is an intangible influence that can have a large and immediate impact on share price. Of course, some portion of market confidence is driven by the overall state of the market and the industry, and is not under the direct control of management. But, to a significant degree, this factor is a reflection of management integrity. As the events surrounding Enron made clear, the absence of integrity can undermine shareholder value more radically than any competitor's action or market fluctuation.

One of the best measures of a company's management integrity is its track record in stakeholder value creation. The investment research company Innovest specializes in analyzing companies' environmental, social, and governance performance and the resulting impact on shareholder value. Using sectoral analyses, Innovest finds a consistent correlation between stakeholder performance and sustained growth in shareholder value.[16]

Discipline 5 leads to the strategic and financial justification for the value creation initiatives. It is what creates cross-functional executive alignment regarding justification, next steps, and roles during implementation.

Challenges

- Obtaining input and buy-in from line management and financial heads

- Developing the business logic for the implications of stakeholder value for shareholder value. For example, answering the question "why does rehabilitating an industrial site or greening a building beyond what is required by law create shareholder value rather than cost the company money?"

- Gathering hard data for financial calculations

- Avoiding the perception that ethics is being monetized

- Projecting the costs and benefits in a meaningful way, given the timing and complexity of implementation when multiple stakeholders are involved

- To the extent possible, assigning a monetary value for each initiative, including the impact of stakeholder value on shareholder value

- Obtaining input and buy-in from the line managers who will ultimately be accountable for delivering the results

Discipline 6: Capture the value

Discipline 6 enables managers to deliver the promised results. It embeds social and environmental initiatives into the organization with cross-functional implementation teams—or sustainable value networks—that include key external stakeholders.

Sustainable value capture requires greater alignment with external players along the end-to-end value chain than what many managers are used to. It requires more transparency and often additional education about the environmental and social issues, and what these issues mean in business terms. Leading companies implementing sustainable value initiatives need to consider fresh tactics such as lobbying government to *raise* environmental performance standards (rather than slowing down legislation as is the case in business-as-usual). New types of collaboration are required, such as R&D and sales working together to redesign products to offer greater environmental benefits as a way to differentiate the company's offerings.

This discipline requires the managers responsible for implementation to work collaboratively with stakeholders in a way that promotes learning while advancing existing business priorities. It requires the initiatives to be integrated into management and accountability structures and processes. It establishes two-way communication mechanisms and action meetings to engage key stakeholders throughout the implementation process.

Stakeholder value is thus captured as part of how the core business value is delivered. Rather than a parallel Total Quality Environmental Management (TQEM) effort, environmental efficiencies are integrated into Six Sigma and other lean management systems for supply chain optimization.

Sustainable value leadership

- Has CEO support
- Involves a guiding coalition or other group of key influencers that usually includes senior operating executives
- Is carried out by cross-functional networks with external engagement of key stakeholders throughout the whole system
- Goes beyond incremental value opportunities to include breakthrough innovations and game-changing moves

Sustainable value management

- Implementation and governance structures effectively set priorities and include those with organizational responsibility for implementing stakeholder value initiatives
- A process exists for managing progress and meeting milestones
- Sustainable value initiatives are integrated with Six Sigma and/or other key sources of value capture

Discipline 6 requires stakeholder management and engagement as part of the normal course of business. It benefits from continual testing: piloting new ideas, developing short-term wins, and learning from successes and failures. The added complexity of multiple stakeholders makes the classic "golden rules" of leadership and management all the more relevant.

Many of the best tools for Discipline 6 are those already in use adapted to include stakeholder as well as shareholder perspectives. These might include:

- Six Sigma and lean management programs
- Total Quality Management (TQM)
- Supply chain integration
- Customer relationship management (CRM)
- Re-engineering

These traditional business approaches benefit from softer, culture-change techniques where external stakeholders and social or environmental issues are introduced. Culture-change approaches to implementing sustainable value initiatives can involve stakeholder surveys, focus groups, and advisory councils to help shape leadership development programs or training programs focused on the mind-sets and behaviors of executives in the organization.

The approach should be to adopt the tools that your organization has already used successfully. Where gaps exist, managers should look to best-practice tools adapted to their particular situation.

Challenges

- Sustainable value teams that pursue environmental and social initiatives for their own sake, instead of for the sake of creating business value, can lose momentum as the business rationale diminishes. For example, reducing the amount of product packaging is a valued environmental goal but it is unlikely to receive support from line management unless it is carried out in pursuit of business priorities such as reducing waste or increasing shelf loads

- A lack of CEO and senior-level support, or having a key level of line management out of the loop, can turn the effort into a parallel initiative with insufficient buy-in from operations

- The hand-off between the designers and the implementers can be confusing because of the many stakeholders involved

- Results take too long to see, so the organization loses interest

- It can be difficult to gain the appropriate degree of involvement from stakeholders

- Working with stakeholders can become an unproductive turf war rather than a collaboration that promotes learning and advances business priorities

- The initiatives may not be well integrated into existing management and accountability structures and processes

- The implementation of the initiatives may suffer from a lack of ongoing communication and engagement with key stakeholders

Discipline 7: Validate results and capture learning

This discipline is the systematic results tracking and feedback loop that enables learning and continual improvement in the organization. The metrics used in Discipline 1 to establish a baseline assessment of shareholder and stakeholder value are further developed to measure progress. A key component of success is sharing what has been learned throughout the larger system—working with suppliers, customers, and other value chain partners to educate them on the business opportunities; as well as to be educated by them about the environmental and social dimensions of the company's activities.

Learning can be shared formally in sustainable value networks designed to advance specific initiatives. These networks look for ways to encourage suppliers and other business partners to improve sustainability performance while increasing profits. New metrics can be developed such as product scorecards that include explicit measures of stakeholder value.

A scorecard for evaluating a supplier and its product might include the following example metrics:

- Will the company take the product back for recycling?

- How many grams of toxic chemicals are there per pound of product?

- What is the percentage of recycled/renewable materials (by weight)?

- Is the product Energy Star certified or equivalent?

- What is the ratio of package volume to product volume?

- What percentage of product packaging by weight is PVC?

Such supplier and product scorecards can be used to rate inputs, product designs, and value chain partners. Procurement specialists and product designers can use the scorecard metrics to make more informed design and product purchase decisions. As a result of using the scorecards, the company's suppliers and other business partners will have new incentives to change their practices.

Key components of this discipline include:

- Choosing a limited set of key attributes of products or value chain partners that determine stakeholder-related business risks and opportunities

- Including those attributes that NGOs and other stakeholders view as the key issues related to that product or value chain activity. (For instance, a product scorecard for PCs and cellphone handsets that did not address the need for product take-back by the manufacturer to avoid electronics waste going to landfills would be perceived as a big miss)

- Assessing actual progress in achieving targets regularly defined in the business case

- Holding learning-focused reviews of the initiatives to assess potential barriers to value realization and revise initiative approaches as needed

- Reviewing many initiative results against the overall sustainable value goals and refining the goals as appropriate

In addition to tracking results, this process should capture lessons learned about the process of sustainable value creation in order to refine the organization's tools, processes, and frameworks—in particular regarding stakeholder dialog, stakeholder value assessment, and business case development.

One of the biggest challenges in this discipline is integrating a broader set of stakeholder metrics into operations. If the company already uses a balanced scorecard approach to measurement where economic stakeholders such as customers and supply chain partners are represented, then extending this scorecard to include social and environmental performance measures will be easier.

A critical success factor in this discipline is to engage the CFO organization in the process of broadening the metrics used to assess and report shareholder value, including strategic value (the option value of R&D and learning investments). Another success factor is embedding stakeholder performance tracking and reporting in the line organizations.

Challenges

- Tailoring the metrics to the business and introducing them at the right time. Introducing stakeholder metrics too early can be a distraction as managers struggle to understand why they are being asked to modify performance measures

- Getting line management to adopt new metrics that include stakeholder performance

- Getting the CFO organization fully engaged

- Getting the CFO organization to broaden the metrics used to assess and report shareholder value (for example, having financial decision-makers include strategic value and market confidence in valuing investment proposals)

- Creating a learning culture and valuing effective learning conversations among all team members

Discipline 8: Build sustainable value organizational capacity

Discipline 8 is a meta-discipline focused on developing the mind-set and organizational capabilities needed to embed a sustainable value perspective into the business. Managers in leading organizations are increasingly being required to incorporate stakeholder issues into their day-to-day activities, rather than delegate them to EH&S or CSR specialists. This shift in mind-set requires greater accountability for stakeholder impacts along the full value chain, covering supply chain activities that managers have historically considered to be outside the company's responsibility. Mattel's failure in September 2007 to identify leaded paint in toys manufactured for the company in China is just the latest in a long list of environmental and social debacles along supply chains overseas.

Discipline 8 requires the organization to embed new practices such as stakeholder engagement and new measurement systems such as expanding a balanced scorecard to include stakeholder value metrics. Achieving competence in these areas demands a coherent, consistent, and organized approach to expanding the value horizon not only within each discipline but also across disciplines.

The outcome of this discipline is an organization skilled at each of the preceding seven disciplines. Discipline 8 promotes a new way of thinking about value creation, systematically bringing a stakeholder perspective into the firm. Every action and interaction supports a sustainable value approach to business.

The competencies required to promote and strengthen each of the first seven disciplines are listed on the following pages.

Building organizational capacity for Discipline 1—understand current value position

- Frame the value creation problem in a way that sees stakeholders and their environmental and social issues as business opportunities rather than threats

- Broaden what managers consider to be the boundaries of business. The new boundaries require executives to manage value chain impacts from raw materials to product end-of-life; it requires them to listen to societal stakeholders that they previously may have considered to be marginal or irrelevant to business decision-making; and it implies knowledge of environmental and social issues that many managers may simply not have

- Offer executive education on the business logic of sustainable value. Frame the business logic in terms of the changing competitive environment in which stakeholders have new-found power to influence business outcomes

- Use whole-systems thinking in assessing stakeholder impacts

Building organizational capacity for Discipline 2—anticipate future expectations

- Commit to investing the time and energy to explore sustainability trends and emerging issues. Use scenario planning not as an exercise in predicting the future but instead as a way to ready the organization for sustainability-driven disruptive change

- Establish a regular process for scanning emerging issues that include environmental and social factors

- Strengthen the ability to recognize which environmental and social issues are meaningful for the business

- Create a process for identifying low-probability short-term events and high-probability long-term ones. In scenario building, learn to detach from the business model that generated the company's success in the past and present

Building organizational capacity for Discipline 3—set sustainable value goals

- Set targets that stretch the organization (the sustainable value intent). Go beyond the known solution set

- Look at a broad range of stakeholder groups, and what business benefits they potentially bring, as a way to determine how to set targets and at what level

- Look at all sources of business value, particularly those shaping the business context and the regulatory environment in ways that enable a leading company with superior environmental and social performance to gain competitive advantage

Building organizational capacity for Discipline 4—design value creation initiatives

- Use stakeholder pressures to drive innovation and advance existing business priorities. Stakeholder thinking needs to inform every business decision, every day, at every level of the organization

- Design products and initiatives with new principles such as those of The Natural Step[17] or Bill McDonough and Michael Braungart's

Cradle-to-Cradle: Remaking the Way We Make Things.[18] Design with these new principles integrated into every aspect of core business decision-making

- Get collaboration from value chain partners. Extend stakeholder value criteria to your value chain partners (education and shift of mind-set) in designing the initiatives

Building organizational capacity for Discipline 5—develop the business case

- Use the six levels (Figure 10.4) to simplify the business value analysis and stay focused on the business logic of sustainable value

- Consider the full range of financial value drivers in assessing sustainable value initiatives, not just accounting revenues and costs

- Involve line managers and the CFO organization in obtaining the data and formulating the business case for new initiatives

- Strengthen the ability to project the uncertainties of sustainable value initiatives in financial terms

Building organizational capacity for Discipline 6—capture the value

- Develop team practices for collaborative work. Build project management competence that includes external stakeholders. Create cross-functional teams and develop a process for working across the functions, creating synergies rather than compromises

- Walk the talk: in every aspect of implementation, demonstrate transparency and partnership with key stakeholders

- Ensure that line management integrates the sustainable value initiatives into the business delivery system (and that they are not treated as parallel to the core business)

- Establish two-way communication mechanisms and action meetings to engage key stakeholders throughout the implementation process

Building organizational capacity for Discipline 7—validate results and capture learning

- Familiarize managers with the broad array of emerging stakeholder metrics. Learn about the stakeholder measures that are relevant to the specific sector and company circumstances

- Focus on the measures of stakeholder value that are significant out of the large number of possible impacts, indicators, and metrics

- Link quantified stakeholder value to shareholder value in a way that is compelling to line and financial management

Discipline 8 is a meta-discipline and as such does not have organizational competencies other than the ability to manage change effectively. The following chapter presents sustainable value from a change management perspective.

11

Putting it all together

The eight disciplines fit into a change management framework designed to deal with business discontinuities and, in many cases, disruptive innovation. In this chapter, the backbone of change management has been adapted to the specific challenges presented by a multi-stakeholder environment and revised assumptions about business's role in society. A distinction is made between incremental and breakthrough value opportunities. Sustainability challenges such as climate change and global poverty can require companies to fundamentally redesign their products and, in many cases, their underlying business models. A failure by industry leaders to pursue radical change may not only lead to growing societal problems; it may also represent significant lost business opportunities.

What is unique about the sustainable value change process centers around the role of stakeholders—economic stakeholders such as customers and societal ones such as local communities and NGOs. Working with stakeholders means learning to identify which ones are key to your organization's success and which are not. It calls for new skills to assess your company's stakeholder impacts and to understand what those impacts mean in terms of business risks and opportunities. Partnering with societal stakeholders implies also a willingness to accept diverse points of view, some of which may initially seem irrelevant to business but prove to be a harbinger of future key success factors.

A manufacturing facility's impacts on a local community might include jobs, economic growth, and taxes but also depletion of water resources and chemical safety risks. These negative impacts—if not handled appropriately—may lead to strikes, non-renewal of permits, and reputation damage. They represent significant business risks. On the other hand, the responsible use of water and the elimination of chemical safety risks may lead to faster permit renewals and the ability to attract and retain local talent. These are significant business opportunities. In many organizations, managers may simply not have considered such stakeholder issues to be relevant to business.

A stakeholder-centric change management process begins with what is called here "stakeholder discovery." The process then moves into a collaborative phase, involving partnerships with external stakeholders, to set the sustainable value intent. From the sustainable value intent flows the design of sustainable value initiatives, which then require organizational engagement to implement them, using feedback loops that ensure alignment of the whole system. Finally, results tracking and verification allow management to know that the promised results are being delivered. The overall target is a better-performing company in a more sustainable society.

The following pages describe the key change management phases of sustainable value creation and provide examples and further tools for the practitioner.

Stakeholder discovery

The discovery phase reorganizes the managerial view of stakeholders, moving them from outside the sphere of business to giving them a central role in it. It requires managers to identify key stakeholder groups and assess the company's economic, social, and environmental impacts on these groups throughout the value chain. In effect, stakeholder value for business comes to represent the market internalization of a social and ecological dimension that was viewed, until recently, as external to business.

In this phase, assessing stakeholder value is not just about seeing more but about seeing differently. A view of the world centered on sustainable value creation typically involves four key elements that shape how stakeholders are viewed in the business system:

- **Broad vision.** Seeing all stakeholders in a global systems context

- **Foresight.** Sensing emerging issues as perceived by stakeholders and tracing potential impacts as experienced by them

- **Deep understanding.** Listening for stakeholder concerns and needs. This is different from stakeholder input. Fully listening to stakeholders requires dialog and softer skills such as empathy and emotional intelligence

- **Integrity of action.** Walking the talk to create value for shareholders and stakeholders

Stakeholder discovery has an information component: providing executives with better and more up-to-date information about emerging issues such as climate change and the price of CO_2 emissions, or the implications of the Alien Torts Act for human rights abuses. It also has an experiential and emotional component that transforms how executives relate to social and environmental responsibility. In *The Heart of Change*,[1] Professor John Kotter says:

> People change what they do less because they are given an analysis that shifts their thinking than because they are shown a truth that influences their feelings.

This observation applies particularly well to the challenge of stakeholder discovery, because this phase requires a deep shift in how businesspeople relate to the world around them.

The analytic case for a hydrogen fuel cell car pales in comparison with actually getting into a quiet, emissions-free vehicle that offers increased safety, comfort, and personalized design—and then imagining how the world would look if all vehicles were like that. The financial logic for moving from conventional cotton farming to organic cotton is a weaker motivator than walking through a conventional cotton field and seeing the scorched earth or feeling itchy eyes and burning skin from the harsh agricultural chemicals used.

The stakeholder discovery phase aligns larger issues of sustainability with business purpose. An example of discovery is deep dialog with stakeholders such as employees and local communities about the company's environmental and social impacts. Dow Chemical, for instance, listens to its stakeholders through an independent 12-member corporate environmental advisory council whose purpose is to increase understanding of diverse viewpoints through active stakeholder partnership and dialog.

Social and environmental impacts require the use of different drivers and measures than those used to quantify the financial impacts of a business in the traditional perspective. Ben Cohen, one of the founders of Ben & Jerry's, said:

> In a business, the only way to measure success is to count the money you have at the end of the year. Since that is the only thing that is measured, it is the only aim that the people involved in a business are motivated to achieve.

In a world where what gets measured gets managed, stakeholder performance requires its own set of metrics.

For many managers who are assessing the shareholder value of social and environmental projects, economic value added and its four drivers (profitability, capital efficiency, cost of capital, and growth) are the most commonly used measures. However, discounted cash flow is insufficient for many projects involving emerging issues and stakeholder impacts because of the uncertainty of future cash flow impacts.

Strategic value assessed through real options is a powerful way to account for the foresight of management teams in creating opportunities and managing risks from emerging issues that might threaten shareholder value. Market confidence is an intangible influence that can have a large and immediate impact on share price. As noted previously, some portion of market confidence is driven by the overall state of the market and the industry, and is not under direct control of management. But, to a significant degree, this factor is a reflection of management integrity. One of the best measures of a company's integrity is its track record in managing stakeholder impacts.

What does the organization look like at the end of the stakeholder discovery phase? If it has done an effective job of assessing current and future stakeholder impacts and value, it knows that it needs to shift strategically but it doesn't necessarily know what this strategy will look like. The phase of setting the strategic intent addresses this next set of objectives.

Collaboratively setting the sustainable value intent

The next step is the co-creation of the sustainable value intent in partnership with external stakeholders who are able to represent the whole system. The competencies and tools needed to create the intent are primarily those of Discipline 3. Once the intent is established, the company needs to develop a strategy to move the business to the win–win quadrant, where value is created for both shareholders and stakeholders. This strategy includes an agreed roadmap for how to achieve the intent. It includes:

- A strategic fact base
- Sustainable value goals and objectives
- A prioritized set of capacity gaps
- A prioritized set of sustainable value creation initiatives
- Open issues to address including those requiring additional stakeholder consultation
- The development of stakeholder metrics tailored to the value chain

A whole-system approach captures all the key stakeholder issues and interests relative to the business. Stakeholder summits that co-create the strategic intent are supplemented by fact-finding and analysis to identify

---

Key questions

- What is our sustainable value vision?
- How can we address social impacts, challenges, and future expectations while advancing existing business priorities?
- How should we identify and manage emerging stakeholder issues?
- How should we measure success?
- What initiatives should we pursue?
- What capabilities do we need?
- What are new sources of sustainable value (i.e. where is shareholder value not created at the expense of stakeholder value)?

and assess specific initiatives, identify capability gaps to be filled, and develop an action plan and implementation process. In strategy development, the key step is to give flesh and bones to the sustainable value vision.

Disciplines 3 and 4 are critical to answering the questions shown in the box above. In this phase, managers are still exploring new opportunities. As shown in Figure 11.1, the first part of the change management process is expansive and divergent. In the next phase, managers begin to make choices, moving into a decisive and convergent mode.

In Figure 11.1, managers begin by selecting the company's key stakeholders and then engaging with them. Managers explore stakeholder issues and interests along the value chain and how the company is impacting those issues and interests. They expand the scope of business risk and opportunity before choosing which value creation initiatives to focus on. They make the business case for those initiatives, obtain the necessary resources (including what is required for stakeholder alignment), and then implement the initiatives.

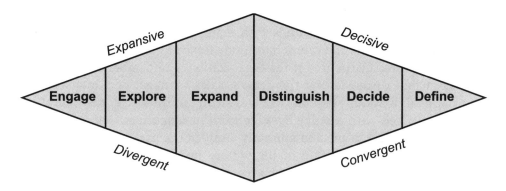

FIGURE 11.1 The stakeholder value assessment process[2]

Value creation initiatives

Value creation initiatives convert the vision, strategic objectives, and values of a company into tangible business results. It is useful to frame sustainable value initiatives in terms of the levels of strategic focus and the financial value drivers that capture the full range of value opportunities.

The role of intangibles and real options are often overlooked by sustainability champions, yet are of heightened interest given the uncertainties of such sustainability-related events as mandatory CO_2 cap-and-trade schemes or possibly even a carbon tax at some point in the future. When an energy company invests in solar and wind technology, it is in effect creating a real option for itself in case future market conditions mandate a rapid move into non-fossil-fuel markets. Disciplines 4 and 5 are the essential competencies here.

Organizational engagement

Organizational engagement allows key managers throughout the company to understand and align with the sustainable value creation vision of the senior leadership. Engaging line management is critical to moving the business case from an analytic exercise to specific plans and actions in the business units.

The business world abounds with examples of organizations in which vision statements and value charters are issued by senior executives, only to be ignored by the rest of the organization. I remember one particular day when I was visiting the general sales manager of a major multinational in Miami, Florida. As I was sitting in his office, the interoffice mail arrived with a bulky package from headquarters. My host smiled across the desk at me and promptly dumped the package unopened into his wastebasket. He said mailings from headquarters were a waste of time. Imagine if that package had contained a newly formulated strategy for the company with direct consequences for how he was to do his job!

More common are vision statements distributed in interoffice memos or framed on office walls for general consumption. Even if employees do read these declarations of intent, the words have little value beyond the paper they are printed on. For managers to buy into sustainable value creation—particularly managers in business units charged with running the day-to-day operations, who may view anything beyond short-term profit as a distraction from the business of business—they must be given an opportunity to engage in the business logic of stakeholder performance. Organizational alignment is not so much about reinventing the company's strategic intent and developing strategy as it is about grappling with the strategy once senior leadership is aligned.

Shared values reflect the behavioral aspirations of the organization. They are a preferred vehicle for diffusing corporate responsibility throughout the organization. Prescribing behavior or technical compliance to corporate responsibility leads to weak leadership and is often cost-prohibitive. A process to help many employees see the world in a new way enables more profitable integration of corporate responsibility.

"What is evoked from within need not be imposed from above." Once employees are aware of and connected to stakeholder concerns, most will naturally try to satisfy them in the conduct of their work—just as when they are aware of customer requirements, they naturally strive to satisfy them.

Shared values relate the whole and the parts—how people, teams, and business units intend to conduct themselves—in pursuit of the company's strategy. They are critical to aligning the business unit managers with the overall direction of the company. Organizational alignment requires a conscious refashioning of focus on a sustainable future—the company's enhanced strategic intent.

By its nature, sustainable value creation requires a cross-functional, cross-border, multi-level engagement of the organization. A guiding coalition composed of senior managers from operations, finance, product design, and other key functional areas, as well as external stakeholders, is critical to engage the organization in implementing the value creation initiatives. Disciplines 6 and 7 (see Chapter 10) provide the guiding tools to build the organizational engagement needed.

Results tracking and verification

If it is true that what gets measured gets managed, then quantifying the benefits of sustainability is an essential task for managers committed to integrating sustainability into the bottom line. There are two levels of tracking and verifying results: the project level and the company-wide level.

At the project level, benefits are typically cost reductions and materials savings. For example, switching to diesel engines and reducing greenhouse gas emissions while lowering fuel and vehicle maintenance costs, or re-engineering a manufacturing process to reduce energy and decrease raw material inputs. Project-level work can also lead to product or service redesign for a differentiation strategy based on environmental or social benefits.

At the company-wide level, benefits are more easily related to sustainability brand value, improved customer mix, and other top-line revenue growth opportunities. The relationship with government authorities allows the company to help shape environmental regulations in its favor based on competitively superior environmental performance.

In this step, budget priorities that reflect the sustainable value intent and enable the chosen initiatives are developed. The goal is to initiate quick-win projects that start delivering value within the fiscal year. Results at 30, 60, and 90 days are targeted and quantified in financial terms. These are complemented by longer-term innovation projects that enable the company to advance its financial, environmental, and social performance.

To maximize the benefits of sustainable value initiatives, they must be communicated both internally and externally. Companies can develop separate sustainability reports or, better yet, integrate new content about sustainability performance into the Annual Report.

A concluding distinction—incremental versus breakthrough sustainable value

A growing number of global industry leaders are adopting elements of the sustainable value model as an integral part of their strategy and operations.

Because many of the underlying sustainability issues such as climate change and global poverty demand radical solutions from a stakeholder perspective, these industry leaders are faced with the need for potentially disruptive changes to the way they do business. Yet the built-in tendency in many companies is to make incremental changes that are incapable of producing enduring benefits for stakeholders or shareholders. The problem is particularly acute for mainstream legacy players.[3]

When sustainability initiatives are incremental and remedial in nature, they often fail to provide enduring solutions for stakeholders, instead focusing on cosmetic outcomes or band-aid solutions that only postpone inevitable breakdown. Incremental sustainability initiatives are typically driven by a desire to manage risks, by the search for process efficiency, or by product and market extensions that incrementally "green" an existing offering. Rather than pursue disruptive innovation, managers prefer to tweak their current business model or, in the worse cases, conduct public relations campaigns that merely reframe what they are already doing.

Leading companies that pursue breakthrough change have the opportunity to make a meaningful difference in how environmental and social challenges are addressed. Perhaps more significantly, they may be able to seize huge business opportunities.

We believe this distinction is a timely one given the rapid adoption of sustainability in business. The task for management is no longer to decide whether to integrate sustainability thinking into business decisions or even how to identify and implement sustainability initiatives. The next wave of sustainability practices will require a better understanding of the interplay between business and the environment, and a more nuanced approach to taking action to create enduring value for stakeholders and shareholders.

For managers to obtain the benefits from sustainable value strategies, they will need new competencies, including the ability to distinguish material (substantive) stakeholder impacts and their degree of importance to shareholder value. In the new competitive environment rich in stakeholder activism, environmental and social impacts that visibly damage human health or the environment represent growing and often hidden business liabilities. Underperformance relative to peers on such key environmental performance factors represent lost business opportunities.

Managers will need to set new design criteria for their supply chains and products or services. The criteria will need to reduce design elements that matter less to customers and increase environmental sustainability factors that customers care about or would care about if they were fully informed. With the new design criteria, the management challenge becomes how to innovate in ways that create value for stakeholders and shareholders.

Figure 11.2 shows the two types of value creation opportunities: incremental and breakthrough, with revenue and cost drivers for each case, as well as success requirements.

Breakthrough sustainable value strategies require disruptive innovations and game-changing moves, such as business initiatives capable of serving markets for the four billion poor living on less than $4 a day. In most cases they will require a fundamental redesign of all major activities along the value chain, with vastly lower energy and materials intensity, extensive partnerships with government and the public sector, the

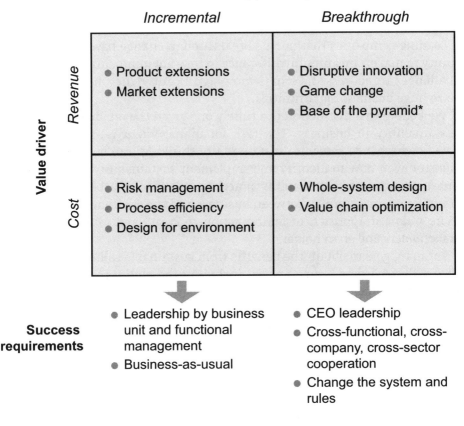

Type of value creation opportunity

	Incremental	*Breakthrough*
Revenue	• Product extensions • Market extensions	• Disruptive innovation • Game change • Base of the pyramid*
Cost	• Risk management • Process efficiency • Design for environment	• Whole-system design • Value chain optimization

Value driver (left axis)

| **Success requirements** | • Leadership by business unit and functional management
• Business-as-usual | • CEO leadership
• Cross-functional, cross-company, cross-sector cooperation
• Change the system and rules |

* Low-income consumers in emerging markets

FIGURE 11.2 **Incremental versus breakthrough**

Source: Blu Skye Sustainability Consulting

inclusion of low-income consumers in emerging markets, and performance metrics that include value created or destroyed for society. As shown in Figure 11.2, such breakthrough value opportunities will require a whole-system transformation and involve value chain optimization that extends from raw materials to product end-of-life. Success requirements for breakthrough sustainable value initiatives include CEO leadership with cross-functional, cross-company, and cross-sector cooperation. Accountability and risk taking become essential at every level of the organization.

Sustainable value creation rooted in breakthrough innovation ultimately leads to a transformation in the business system with greater upside potential, but also more risk, for both shareholders and stakeholders.

Conclusion

The following summary of "lessons learned" reflects key insights from global industry leaders and the work of many managers who have tackled sustainable value in their own organizations.

Sustainability provides new insights into business strategy and the competitive environment

Sustainability is a "lens" through which line managers can innovate along their extended supply chains. It is not about trade-offs, and recent corporate experience proves time and again that sustainability-based investments can have paybacks of a year or less. Moral responsibility remains the foundation for sustainability action, but not the primary motivator. Sustainability champions need to acquire the skills to engage senior executives and line managers by demonstrating that sustainability can profitably advance key business priorities.

Sustainability solutions require collaboration with key stakeholders

Partnering with stakeholders can reduce opposition and bring new knowledge. Effective stakeholder relationships must take into account perceptions and emotions. Companies cannot rely solely on their own scientific or technical arguments for why their impacts on society are safe for human health and the environment. Countering emotional fear with cold analytic logic only worsens the mistrust between companies and their stakeholders. On the other hand, executives need to be able to distinguish between activists who wage destructive campaigns from those who are interested in constructively shaping the future. Managers must accept that they cannot please all stakeholders all the time.

Sustainability solutions require new organizational competencies

New leadership skills include assessing and managing stakeholder impacts along the supply chain. Business solutions that involve the stakeholder dimension require the ability to build relationships with the key players along the supply chain. Decisions at any point of the value chain must reflect the interests of the whole. Innovations that create benefits for the whole system are likely to be adopted faster and remain longer in place.

Companies that lack the organizational capacity for listening and empathy must strengthen their ability to reach out to stakeholder groups, particularly those that are seen as very different from the corporate mold. New supporting activities for the organization include social marketing, sales training, and government lobbying to increase environmental and social regulation in the company's favor.

Leading companies that succeed in meeting the sustainable value challenge are turning environmental and social problems into new business opportunities. They are contributing positively to society in ways that create a unique and inimitable source of competitive advantage.

Postscript

Business as an Agent of World Benefit: How the Holy Grail of business—innovation—can be magnified through the power of sustainable value creation

Professor David Cooperrider, Founder and Chairman, Center of Business as an Agent of World Benefit, with Ante Glavas, Executive Director, and Nadya Zhexembayeva, Associate Director

It's not usual for a conservative, financially driven, $10-billion-dollar-a-year multinational—a dependable, high performance company which has increased annual dividends paid to shareholders for 51 consecutive years (among the top five longest-running dividend increase records in the S&P 500 index)—to call together the largest corporate strategy summit in its history in order to focus on "the ten largest global problems facing humankind." The key question:

"How might we turn these social and global environmental issues into strategic business opportunities to ignite innovation in new products and operations, open new unexpected markets, ignite customer passion and loyalty, turn on and energize an entire workforce, accelerate learning, build better supply chains, reduce risks, radically bring down energy costs, and produce tangible and intangible value such as brand loyalty and higher market cap—and build a safer, more secure, better world?"

By the end of the three-day session, the grey pinstripes were replaced with business casuals, and spontaneous cheers echoed as a new vision of the company's future—as a solution provider to the ten largest global challenges facing humankind—began to take shape and a substantive form.

The chief architect of the summit wanted to find a way to connect and unify a totally diversified global company, and to turn on and elevate the imagination and passion of an entire 57,000 workforce leading, ultimately, to a whole new magnitude of business innovation. The meeting was top secret, and still is for proprietary and competitive advantage reasons, until the strategy package is completely bundled and ready for prime time.

What's going on here? This is a company near the top of Barron's list of 500 Best Performing Companies for its superior financial management based on several factors:

- The company's stock performance

- The median cash flow return on investment for the past three years and cash flow return on investment for the current year compared with the three-year historical median

- Sales growth over the latest fiscal year adjusted for acquisitions and divestitures

- Cash flow return on equity

Again, it's not usual for a firm such as this to so radically alter its long-term strategy, business identity, and mission. But these are not ordinary times.

Chris Laszlo's message is huge and simple: we are on the eve of one of the greatest revolutions in management history, an era of deep-seated transformation, where "sustainable value creation" is and can emerge as the most powerful unifying thread for propelling industry-leading innovation in complete and simultaneous convergence with solutions to the call of our times. In *Sustainable Value*, Chris Laszlo makes the vital point not with abstractions but with the real thing—inside stories from some of the largest corporations in the world, and with frameworks, tools, and methods that take sustainable value creation out of the theoretical to the concrete. This volume is a masterful synthesis—part novel and part executive briefing—a refreshing kind of prophetic pragmatism, helping leaders anticipate and see the future in the texture of the actual. Chris Laszlo speaks with resounding clarity; he speaks directly to the living challenges, the real dilemmas, and haunting questions of CEOs everywhere.

Chris Laszlo calmly predicts that, over time, mainstream business will pursue sustainability performance when it advances their business priorities. And that doing good and doing well is increasingly the smartest way to do business, if you have the knowledge and competencies to turn eco-imagination and social entrepreneurship into an innovation engine.

Where can executives go for leadership education in sustainable value creation?

We were absolutely thrilled when Chris Laszlo joined our faculty for executive education at Case Western Reserve University to help us found and create an applied research center for sustainable value creation at the Weatherhead School of Management—a school the Aspen Institute singled out as "on the cutting edge."

While it is beyond the scope or purpose of this postscript to give a full description of the Center for Business as an Agent of World Benefit (BAWB), we accepted Chris Laszlo's invitation to reflect for a moment on the center from the perspective of the main thesis of his book. And it's true: even the remarkable genesis of BAWB is a telling tale for, in fact, the domain of sustainable value creation is moving faster than any management school can keep up with.

In 2004, Kofi Annan, Secretary-General of the United Nations, called us at the Weatherhead School of Management. In many ways it was an astonishing call. Having been briefed on the power of the large group Appreciative Inquiry Summit method, the Secretary-General decided that it could be the best method to advance the UN Global Compact. In short, our team was invited to facilitate what became the largest meeting in history between the UN and hundreds of CEOs, from companies such as Hewlett Packard, Green Mountain Coffee Roasters, Nokia, Microsoft, Lafarge, Novartis, Novo Nordisk, Tata, and many others. The summit was an exploration into the next phases of global corporate citizenship, where Kofi Annan reached out his hand to the business leaders and said: "Let us choose to unite the strengths of markets with the power of universal ideals, let us choose to reconcile the forces of private entrepreneurship with needs of the disadvantaged and the well-being of future generations."

The summit was powerful. And three years later a second summit took place. During the time between those world summits, an explosion of energy occurred: as of this moment there are now 4,000 companies (mostly multinationals) that are part of the UN Global Compact's new corporate citizenship movement.

But Chris Laszlo taught us, when we were co-creating the BAWB Center that the word "citizenship" was "off." In the world of ideas, as Thomas Friedman wrote, to name something is to own it: "if you can name an issue, you can own the issue." Like Freidman's analysis of the word "green," the one thing that always struck us about the term "corporate citizenship" was the degree to which, for so many years, it was defined as the opposite of the real business. Opponents especially, people who wanted to disparage it, would roll their eyes if you brought it up at a senior executive strategy think-tank, defining it as "charity," "expensive regulatory compliance," "liberal," "a side-line distraction," and "vaguely relevant."

Well it's time to rename "corporate citizenship"—this is what Chris Laszlo said to us. We need to reposition it as geo-strategic, opportunity-producing, as an innovation turbocharger. It's precisely what's happening—if you really pay attention—to the emerging stars in virtually every industry. Just as the Internet boom sent people scrambling to invest in the next Google, the same thing is now happening to companies that are emerging as pioneers in clean tech, micro-enterprise (eradicating poverty through profitability), and sustainability.

Who is going to surprise us with the next new "Prius," or who will be the next new "Whole Foods" or "Fairmount Minerals"? Likewise, why is there so much investor excitement with paradigm-shifting NanoSolar—with its workforce on fire—and its promise of building a world that is clean and profoundly renewable in its energy options? It's all about sustainable value creation, says Chris Laszlo: it's revolutionary and it is renaming.

At the Case Western Reserve University's Weatherhead School of Management, we believe that management is a matter of world affairs, a noble profession, and that every global and social issue of our day is a business opportunity. The school's interdisciplinary centerpiece for advancing sustainability and social entrepreneurship is the BAWB Center. Through advanced research and tremendously innovative executive education as well as applied sustainable design with whole systems, our passion is to help our partners—corporations, entrepreneurs, and industry associations—succeed and become the top-rated stars in their industries while, at the same time, building a world that is:

- Clean and profoundly renewable in its energy options

- Securer and safer and more than just the one we are inhabiting

- Economically alive with a new spirit of innovation, entrepreneurship, and moral imagination

In the end, the greatest gift that Chris Laszlo leaves us with is a choice. He shows us that sustainable value creation is possible, and that the future is not predicted so much as created. Let us choose. Let us "out-innovate." Let us participate in a task of historic proportion.

What executives can expect from the BAWB Center

An increasing number of senior managers, educators, and researchers are sold on the case for doing well by doing good. They are past the debate of *why* this is something that is needed and have moved on to the question of *how* we do this. Very few institutions offer solutions for the *how* to do well by doing good. At BAWB we provide the *how* through:

1. **Discovering and sharing** existing knowledge about what works—our World Inquiry program has collected the largest collection of best practices in the world with over 4,000 interviews completed, and over 100 stories published. Our BAWB Global Forum, Colloquium series, quarterly newsletters, and other emerging opportunities allow us to disseminate the most potent and valuable know-how on the "how to" of sustainability

2. **Co-learning and co-creating**—our strength is as a convener of multi-stakeholder, complex dialogs using methodologies such as Appreciative Inquiry. For those questions that we do not have the answers to—and many such questions exist due to the field being so young—we bring the leading experts together with business leaders to co-learn and co-create models (for both practice and research) through a learning lab environment

Topic areas

- **Sustainable value**—transforming your business into one that profitably addresses its own unique set of social and/or environmental issues

- **Social entrepreneurship**—starting with social and/or environmental issues to which a business model will be applied so that profit can be made while addressing them

Examples of social and environmental issues that we focus on are poverty, the environment (such as climate change), health, and peace.

Focus areas

- **Practice**—a hands-on approach using whole-systems method-ologies to work with complex, multi-stakeholder issues facing companies in a diverse range of sectors:
  - Discovering and applying what already works
  - Co-creating new innovative solutions for sustainable business

We are working with leading companies, large and small, that are becoming models and benchmarks for other businesses around the world, helping their industries reach a tipping point where management practice is transformed.

- **Education**—through collaboration with leading associations, institutions, networks, and schools, we are working to trans-form management education so as to influence the millions of students graduating from business school each year

- **Research**—developing new models for business that will be used by businesses and taught in schools around the world

To learn more about the BAWB Center and what it can do for you, con-tact:

BAWB, 10900 Euclid Avenue, Cleveland, Ohio 44106-7235

Phone: 216.368.3809

worldbenefit.case.edu

Endnotes

Introduction

1 Sports utility vehicles.

2 C. Holliday, S. Schmidheiny, and P. Watts, *Walking the Talk: The Business Case for Sustainable Development* (Sheffield, UK: Greenleaf Publishing, 2002).

3 S. Hart, *Capitalism at the Crossroads: The Unlimited Business Opportunities in Solving the World's Most Difficult Problems* (Upper Saddle River, NJ: Wharton School Publishing, 2005).

4 R. Willard, *The Next Sustainability Wave: Building Room Buy-in* (Gabriola Island, BC: New Society Publishers, 2005).

5 D. Esty and A. Wilson, *Green to Gold: How Smart Companies Use Environmental Strategy to Innovate, Create Value, and Build Competitive Advantage* (New Haven, CT: Yale University Press, 2006).

6 A. Hoffman, *Competitive Environmental Strategy: A Guide to the Changing Business Landscape* (Washington, DC: Island Press, 2000).

7 F. Reinhardt, *Down to Earth: Applying Business Principles to Environmental Management* (Boston, MA: Harvard Business School Press, 1999).

8 W. Blackburn, *The Sustainability Handbook: The Complete Management Guide to Achieving Social, Economic and Environmental Responsibility* (London: Earthscan Publications, 2007).

9 R. Doppelt, *Leading Change toward Sustainability: A Change-Management Guide for Business, Government and Civil Society* (Sheffield, UK: Greenleaf Publishing, 2003).

Chapter 2

1 Patagonia and others pioneered the use of organic cotton in clothing apparel, but Wal-Mart is the first to commercialize it in mainstream channels and to seek price parity with conventional cotton products. See, for example, C. Laszlo, *The Sustainable Company: How to Create Lasting Value through Social and Environmental Value* (Washington, DC: Island Press, 2003): chapter 6.

Chapter 3

1 For one of the best-selling strategy books of 2006, see W. Chan Kim and R. Mauborgne, *Blue Ocean Strategy: How to Create Uncontested Market Space and Make the Competition Irrelevant* (Boston, MA: Harvard Business School Press, 2004). In conversations with the author at INSEAD, Professor Mauborgne readily agreed that sustainability strategies were an excellent application of Blue Ocean thinking.

2 The project descriptions in this section owe much to actual projects undertaken at Interface and Fairmount Minerals—two industry leaders that have embodied sustainable value in recent years.

Chapter 4

1 L. Lindo and Y. Kimura (eds.), THINK: *The First Principle of Business Ethics* (Walter Russell IBM Lecture Series, with a personal introduction by Thomas J. Watson, Sr; Waynesboro, VA: University of Science and Philosophy, 2003).

2 J. Keeble, D. Lyon, D. Vassalo, G. Hedstrom, and H. Sanchez, *How Leading Companies are Using Sustainability-Driven Innovation to Win Tomorrow's Customers* (Boston, MA: Arthur D. Little, 2005).

3 T.L. Friedman, *The World is Flat: A Brief History of the Twenty-first Century* (New York: Farrar, Straus, & Giroux, 2005).

4 From *The Vancouver Sun*, April 24, 2007: "*YouTube* is frequented from everyone to teenagers after school to reporters to customers who can now all see for themselves what West Fraser's logging practices look like," according to the environmental group ForestEthics. "Our staff made [the anti-logging] video sitting at their desks in Vancouver. We were able to do a fly-over of West Fraser's logging operations using Google. We have never been able to do this so quickly before."

5 E. Assadourian, "The Role of Stakeholders," *World Watch Magazine* 18.5 (September/October 2005).

6 At the forefront of activist stakeholders are environmental NGOs, non-profits with social causes, bloggers of various stripes, the media, and investor groups. Distributed Internet-based platforms that are user-driven, such as *YouTube*, also provide a powerful outlet for corporate critics.

Chapter 5

1 From a conversation with the author on January 22, 2007.

Chapter 6

1 Wal-Mart's sustainability strategy was articulated by CEO Lee Scott in a speech on October 24, 2005 ("21st Century Leadership"). For an example of mainstream press reactions, see A. Murray, "Can Wal-Mart Sustain a Softer Edge?" *The Wall Street Journal*, February 8, 2006.

2 *Ibid.*

3 Wal-Mart's sustainability footprint represents the impact it has on the environment in terms of resource use, waste generation, and physical environmental changes. The footprint of Wal-Mart's own operations—running stores
   and operating truck fleets—is far smaller than the footprint of its merchandise
   supply chains including raw materials, manufacturing, and third-party ship-
   ping of the products it purchases.

4 Stakeholders include not only the direct and indirect economic participants in
   the value chain such as suppliers, customers, employees, and shareholders,
   but also includes societal stakeholders, such as local communities, NGOs representing society and the environment, and government agencies and regulators representing the public interest.

5 The Organic Exchange website (www.organicexchange.org/links) gives details
   of resources and links for cotton production and health impacts.

6 See note 1 of Chapter 2.

7 The estimate assumes no increase in fuel costs over time. All figures are esti-
   mates due to the ongoing development of the product.

Chapter 8

1 NAPCOR.

Chapter 9

1 Pioneering works on the rise of stakeholder power in business include: R.E.
   Freeman, *Strategic Management: A Stakeholder Approach* (New York: Basic Books,
   1984); and, more recently: S. Waddock, C. Bodwell, and S.B. Graves, "Responsibility: The New Business Imperative," *Academy of Management Executive* 16.2
   (2002): 132-48.

2 See, for example, J. Hand and B. Lev (eds.), *Intangible Assets: Values, Measures and
   Risks* (Oxford, UK: Oxford University Press, 2003).

3 M.E. Porter, *Competitive Strategy: Techniques for Analyzing Industries and Competitors*
   (New York: The Free Press, 1980).

4 For a discussion of stakeholder engagement practices, see J. Andriof, S. Waddock, B. Husted, and S.S. Rahman, *Unfolding Stakeholder Thinking 2: Relationships,
   Communication, Reporting and Performance* (Sheffield, UK: Greenleaf Publishing,
   2003).

5 Economic value added (EVA®) is a proprietary framework developed by Stern
   Stewart & Co. It is "net operating profit minus an appropriate charge for the
   opportunity cost of all capital invested in an enterprise. As such, EVA is an estimate of true 'economic' profit, or the amount by which earnings exceed or fall
   short of the required minimum rate of return that shareholders and lenders
   could get by investing in other securities of comparable risk." See www.
   sternstewart.com/evaabout/whatis.php (accessed September 3, 2007).

6   The two private equity companies, Kohlberg Kravis Roberts and the Texas Pacific Group, also agreed to: forego TXU's plans to build conventional coal-fired plants in Pennsylvania, Virginia, or any other state; reduce TXU's carbon emissions to 1990 levels by 2020; endorse the platform of the US Climate Action Partnership (USCAP) coalition including federal legislation for a mandatory cap-and-trade system for greenhouse gas emissions; turn TXU into a leader in tackling global warming; tie executive compensation at TXU to climate stewardship; double the company's spending on energy efficiency; and establish a Sustainable Energy Advisory Committee to help the company implement a business model that includes leadership on tackling global warming (source: *Environmental Defense*, March 2007; www.environmentaldefense.org/article.cfm?contentID=6027).

7   "Environmentalists hail takeover plan for Texas utility," *The Boston Globe*, February 26, 2006.

8   M.E. Porter and M.R. Kramer, "The Competitive Advantage of Corporate Philanthropy," *Harvard Business Review*, December 2002.

9   J. Lash and F. Wellington, "Competitive Advantage on a Warming Planet," *Harvard Business Review*, March 2007.

10 "Study: New US Vehicle CO_2 Emissions Dip 3% from 2004 to 2005, but remain up 1.5% since 1990," Green Car Congress, August 31, 2007; www.greencarcongress.com/2007/08/study-new-us-ve.html.

11 Talk at the National Press Club by Jim Olson, former head of external affairs, Toyota Motor North America, on September 16, 2003.

12 A. Ohnsman, "Toyota adds incentives to boost US Prius sales 50%," Bloomberg, February 5, 2007.

13 "Toyota to go all-hybrid by 2020?" C|Net News Blog, May 17, 2007; news.com.com/8301-10784_3-9720051-7.html (accessed September 4, 2007).

14 See A.J. Dunlap with Bob Andelman, *Mean Business: How I Save Bad Companies and Make Good Companies Great* (New York: Fireside, 1997).

15 A. Svendsen, *The Stakeholder Strategy: Profiting from Collaborative Business Relationships* (San Francisco: Berrett-Koehler, 1998).

16 See note 2 above.

17 See also J. Low and P. Cohen Kalafut, *Invisible Advantage: How Intangibles are Driving Business Performance* (Cambridge, MA: Perseus Publishing, 2002).

18 For a discussion of mental models and the mind-set shift required to see the world in a systems perspective, see P.M. Senge, *The Fifth Discipline: The Art and Practice of the Learning Organization* (New York: Currency Doubleday, 1990).

Chapter 10

1   See www.globalreporting.org.
2   See www.unglobalcompact.org.
3   American National Standards Institute and the Institute of Electrical and Electronics Engineers.

4 C. Laszlo and J.-F. Laugel, *Large Scale Organizational Change: An Executive's Guide* (Woburn, MA: Butterworth-Heinemann, 2000).

5 For an excellent account of social activism "flying under the radar" in large organizations, see B. Waugh's *Soul in the Computer: The Story of a Corporate Revolutionary* (Maui, HI: Inner Ocean, 2001).

6 Fairmount Minerals, a world leader in industrial sands, is an example of a company that has successfully used Appreciative Inquiry to involve its entire organization as well as external stakeholders. For more on this company, see www.fairmountminerals.com.

7 J.D. Ludema, "From Deficit Discourse to Vocabularies of Hope: The Power of Appreciation," in D.L. Cooperrider, P.F. Sorensen Jr, D. Whitney, and T.F. Yaeger (eds.), *Appreciative Inquiry: Rethinking Human Organization toward a Positive Theory or Change* (Champaign, IL: Stipes Publishing, 2000).

8 The author wishes to acknowledge Professor David L. Cooperrider for his pioneering vision and early contributions in applying AI to stakeholder engagement for sustainable value creation.

9 D.L. Cooperrider, "Introduction to Appreciative Inquiry," in W. French and C. Bell (eds.), *Organization Development* (Englewood Cliffs, NJ: Prentice Hall, 5th edn, 1995). See also D. Whitney and D.L. Cooperrider, "The Appreciative Inquiry Summit: An Emerging Methodology for Whole System Positive Change," *Journal of the Organization Development Network* 32 (2000): 13-26.

10 C. Laszlo and D.L. Cooperrider, "Design for Sustainable Value: A Whole System Approach," in M. Avital, R.J. Boland, and D.L. Cooperrider (eds.), *Designing Information and Organizations with a Positive Lens* (Advances in Appreciative Inquiry Series, Volume 2; Oxford: Elsevier Science, 2007).

11 Six Sigma is a quality improvement program originally developed by Motorola. Its name comes from a focus on process control to the point of ± six sigma (standard deviations) from a centerline (equivalent to 3.4 defects per million units). To learn more about Six Sigma, see for example *Rath & Strong's Six Sigma Pocket Guide* (Lexington, MA: Rath & Strong, new rev. edn, 2006).

12 See www.climatecrisis.net for more information about Gore's DVD.

13 Based on a conversation between the author and Dawn Rittenhouse, corporate director of sustainable development at DuPont, in early 2007. DuPont is one of the founding members of the US Climate Action Partnership.

14 "In turnaround, industries seek US regulations," *New York Times*, September 16, 2007.

15 The Black–Scholes formula is an option pricing model initially developed by Fischer Black and Myron Scholes for securities options. The model assumes that the price of heavily traded assets follows a geometric Brownian motion with constant drift and volatility. When applied to a stock option, the model incorporates the constant price variation of the stock, the time value of money, the option's strike price and the time to the option's expiry.

16 Relayed to the author in conversations with Hewson Baltzell, president, Innovest Strategic Value Advisors. For more information on Innovest's methodology, see www.innovestgroup.com.

17 For more information, see www.naturalstep.org.
18 B. McDonough and M. Braungart, *Cradle-to-Cradle: Remaking the Way We Make Things* (New York: North Point Press, 2002).

Chapter 11

1 J.P. Kotter and D.S. Cohen, *The Heart of Change: Real-Life Stories of How People Change their Organizations* (Boston, MA: Harvard Business School Press, 2002).
2 The author is grateful to Dave Sherman for introducing this process tool into the sustainable value approach.
3 See, for example, C. Christensen, *The Innovator's Dilemma* (New York: HarperBusiness, 2003).

Index

Page numbers in *italics* indicate figures and tables.